Sculling

Training, Technique & Performance

Paul Thompson

The Crowood Press

First published in 2005 by
The Crowood Press Ltd
Ramsbury, Marlborough
Wiltshire SN8 2HR

www.crowood.com

This impression 2008

British Library Cataloguing-in-Publication Data
A catalogue for this book is available from the British Library.

ISBN 978 1 86126 758 0

Disclaimer
Please note that the author and the publisher of this book are not
responsible in any manner whatsoever for any damage, or injury of
any kind, that may result from practising, or applying, the techniques
and methods and/or following the instructions described in this
publication. Since the physical activities described in this book may
be too strenuous in nature for some readers to engage in safely, it is
essential that a doctor be consulted prior to undertaking training and
sculling activities of any kind.

Throughout this book 'he', 'him' and 'his' are used as neutral
pronouns and as such refer to both males and females.

Illustration Acknowledgements
Photographs by the author.
Line drawings by Ben Webb.

DVD also available, ISBN 978 1 84797 006 0

Typeset and designed by
D & N Publishing
Lambourn Woodlands, Hungerford, Berkshire.

Printed and bound in Spain by GraphyCems.

Contents

Foreword

Sculling has always been a mystery to me. My very first moments in a boat were in a single scull. Feeling a little nervous, I was pushed off into mid-stream and in seconds was rewarded with a swim. But within a few days the confidence had returned and I was getting the very first basics of the discipline.

Sculling has always remained at the very top level an illusion to me. I can do it to a certain standard but I would never have been as successful a sculler as a rower. Part of it is confidence, part technique but, most importantly, I didn't have the desire 'to go it alone'. I never could do the training alone or, indeed, go out to face the world alone. To those that did I will always have time and a huge amount of respect.

Paul Thompson's book, *Sculling: Training, Technique and Performance*, provides the reader not only with the opportunity to understand the principles behind the methods but also presents invaluable advice which will enable the sculler to improve his performance. This volume is a great resource for scullers of all levels who want to combine balance, power and rhythm to make their boat sing.

Sir Matthew Pinsent CBE
British Rower and Quadruple
Olympic Gold Medallist

Dedication

Dedicated to my two boys, Jordan and Lachlan.

Acknowledgements

I would like to thank my partner, Alison, for her unfailing support, ideas, patience and editorial advice; along with my father, John, whose belief, guidance, advice and editorial support have been invaluable.

Thanks also to Miles Forbes-Thomas, Steve Kerr, Craig Williams, Al Smith, Julian Jones, Chris Shambrook, Colin Brown and David Tanner for their chapter reviews and comments, and to Ben Webb who provided some outstanding illustrations, the like of which I could only dream of drawing.

I would also like to thank Lizzie Webb and Harry Wardle for their influence on resistance training for rowers and scullers, and Frances Houghton, Sarah Winckless, Bev Gough and Marcel Hacker for agreeing to be photographed demonstrating the skills that have seen them excel as international athletes. Chris Dodd from the River and Rowing Museum at Henley provided expert guidance and advice for which I am grateful.

I would also like to acknowledge the Amateur Rowing Association and thank them for the use of their educational material.

Finally, I would like to thank all the rowers and scullers I have coached, the coaches I have had and coached with, to whom I owe so much for the enjoyment that sculling, rowing and coaching gives me. Thanks also to those who gave me their time to talk about sculling and to Sir Matthew Pinsent for his Foreword.

Preface

I have been fortunate throughout my rowing and coaching career to have rowed and worked with some exceptionally talented people, not only rowers and coaches but also scientists and medical support staff, who have all shared a burning desire to see rowers and scullers realize their full potential and achieve outstanding performances on the world stage. These colleagues have always challenged my thinking on how to do things differently, rather than simply encouraging me to adopt the 'harder or more of it' philosophy. In this book I have attempted to explain up-to-date and cutting-edge concepts and principles, while giving practical advice on how these may be incorporated into sculling. I should add that I have used these principles with national crews with great success. Whether you are a coach, a keen club member, Masters sculler, national team aspirant, or simply enjoy the occasional recreational scull, I hope to challenge your thinking. My objective in writing this book is to move you closer to attaining the level of sculling to which you aspire and also to increase your enjoyment of the sport even more.

CHAPTER 1
Introduction

Rowing has been used over the centuries for many different purposes, including trade, transport and military operations, as well as for sport and recreation. In Stowe's survey of London in 1598 he reported that 40,000 men made their living on or associated with the Thames.

On British waterways, the watermen would row their wherries. The wherry boat was the water taxi of the pre-steam age, used to transport passengers from one side of the river to the other. The wherry could be sculled by one or two men or rowed by two. It is believed that in the eighteenth century, the Watermen's Company had 10,000 men working the Thames from Gravesend to Richmond.

To celebrate the anniversary of the House of Hanover's accession to the English throne, Thomas Doggett founded a race for apprentice watermen in 1715. The tradition has continued to this day and, as such, it is reputed to be the oldest annual sporting event in the world. Winners of the race become eligible to row the royal barge on state occasions.

During the nineteenth century, the introduction of the sliding seat allowed for greater power in the stroke to come from the use of the legs. Another innovation was the swivelling gate on the outrigger which increased the effective stroke length, and a more efficient hydrodynamic hull shape was developed with

From the water taxi to the racing shell.

the keel inside the boat. As a result, the working boat became faster and sleeker, eventually evolving into the racing shells we see today.

Sculling became a source of great national pride amongst the emerging nations of the British Empire in the nineteenth century. In 1788, the British in the penal colony of New South Wales banned rowing for fear of escape attempts by convicts; however, by 1818 there were organized races among the crews of ships in port. In 1876, Sydneysider Ed Trickett travelled to the mother country to make a challenge for the world sculling title. He won by four lengths and returned home a hero and Australia's first sporting world champion. The Canadians were also boating through their waterways at this time. In London in 1880, Ned Hanlan, who was already the professional champion of England, Canada and the USA, became Canada's first sporting world champion by beating Trickett.

A year prior to the first professional world sculling championship in 1830, the first amateur championship, the Wingfield Sculls, was raced on the Thames. However, while the Wingfield Sculls are still raced today, the professional championships declined in popularity between the two world wars and have not been raced since the 1950s.

By the late nineteenth century, great debate had arisen about the definition of an amateur sportsman. Status rules were devised by bodies such as the Amateur Rowing Association (ARA), formed in 1882, and the Henley Royal Regatta stewards as to who could enter amateur regattas. These rules were primarily concerned with what an amateur was not. He was not a mechanic or a professional; nor could he have taken part in athletic competition for prize money, entrance fees or against a professional. He could not earn a living from teaching or pursue a livelihood associated with athletic endeavours. He definitely was not a manual labourer, employed on or around boats, or received wages. The amateur rowing competitor was also certainly not a woman! The National Amateur Rowing Association, formed in 1890, had a similar definition of the amateur except the manual labour clause was omitted.

The Henley Royal Regatta was first organized by the mayor and people of Henley in 1839 and held in conjunction with a fair and other public amusements. In 1881, it received its royal patronage from HRH Prince Albert, a tradition that has been upheld by each reigning monarch since his death. As the Henley Royal Regatta was instituted prior to the formation of the ARA or the International Rowing Federation (FISA) it has its own rules and does not fall under the jurisdiction of either. It has been organized and run by a self-selecting group of stewards since 1884.

In 1920, the Henley stewards refused the entry of the American amateur J.B. Kelly for the blue ribbon Diamond Sculls event. This may have been because it was rumoured that Kelly had once been an apprentice bricklayer but probably had more to do with the fact that he had a very good chance of winning! Kelly had been looking forward to a showdown with Jack Beresford Jr, the outstanding British sculler of the day, who went on to win that year.

Two months later, in the Olympic final in Antwerp, Kelly won the title by one second. Beresford went on to win medals for Great Britain at five successive Olympic Games between 1920 and 1936. This record was only recently surpassed by Sir Steven Redgrave who won six medals (five of which were gold) from five consecutive Olympics.

Founded in Italy in 1892, FISA is the oldest international sporting federation in the Olympic movement. The first European Championships were held in 1893 and continued until 1962 when the first World Championships were held. Currently, FISA organize world and age-limited championships annually, and scullers and rowers have the opportunity to compete every four years in the Olympic Games.

In 1956, after sixty-five years of co-existence, the ARA and the National Amateur Rowing Association merged to form the Amateur Rowing Association (ARA) as we know it today.

The ARA is the national umbrella organization for a vibrant sport that now has over 20,000 members in more than 500 clubs throughout England. Its many activities include 'Project Oarsome', a programme funded through Sport England and the Henley Stewards' Charitable Trust, that aims to introduce 30,000 youngsters aged between eleven and fourteen to rowing. Its 'World Class Start' programme, also funded by Sport England, has tested around 30,000 school and university students throughout England in a search for the next generation of international rowing and sculling stars.

Scotland has thirty-five rowing clubs with a total membership of approximately 2,000; Wales has twenty-five clubs and Northern Ireland has twenty.

There are many competitions throughout the UK and around the coast in both specially designed and traditional boats. Today, the number of competitors in major events is extremely healthy. The Fours Head, raced in November each year on the Thames, can have up to 500 crews on the water at the same time; while in March the Eights Head races will have 350 women crews entered and the men 450.

The rowing world has often been blessed with two outstanding opposing athletes at the same time and this has produced some epic races on the water. The battle between such individuals can be fascinating; their rivalry and tactics often reflecting their personalities.

'Sculling is like theatre, that's why it's so interesting,' says prominent rowing author, journalist and rowing curator at Henley's River and Rowing Museum, Christopher Dodd. He laments how often scullers that have dominated the world have come in pairs. The American Jack Kelly and Britain's Jack Beresford Jr in the 1920s; the Russian Vjacheslav Ivanov and the colourful Australian Stuart Mackenzie in the 1950s and 1960s; and in the 1970s and early 1980s, West German Peter-Michael Kolbe and the mighty Finnish sculler Pertti Karppinen. Kolbe then went on to fight ferocious battles with East German Thomas Lange when Karppinen left the single and raced in crew boats. More recently, the sculling races have become more and more competitive amongst a number of scullers. The New Zealander, Rob Waddell, the Olympic Champion in 2000 and Xeno Mueller the Swiss Olympic Champion in 1996 who Dodd saw in Atlanta as racing from the start with 'the knowledge he was going to win written on his face.'

The finals of the men's and women's races in the Athens Olympic single scull were both exciting and fiercely competitive events. In the men's race, Norwegian Olaf Tufte came from behind after being passed by the rejuvenated Estonian veteran, Jueri Jaanson. Jaanson led after 1,000m only to fade and be overtaken in the last 300m by Tufte to claim the Olympic title. In the women's final, Belarusian Ekaterina Karsten was going for her third consecutive Olympic title only to be overtaken by German sculler, Katrin Ruschow-Stomporowski, who came from fifth position after 500m.

This book is about sculling, how to improve your technique and coaching skills, but what

> The single sculls race at the World Championships and Olympics is 'the battle of the best individual athletes. The winning single is genuinely the best rower at the regatta' according to Brian Richardson, head coach to the Canadian Olympic rowing team in 1996 and 2004. Richardson coached Canadian Derek Porter to the single sculls world title in 1993 and a silver medal at the Atlanta Olympics.

is it that separates sculling from rowing? Is it merely that the sculler has an oar in each hand and the rower just one oar for both, or does the lone sculler have different character traits to crew boat rowers?

The single sculler has nowhere to hide – he must rely on his own skills, strengths and mental toughness, but the enjoyment of success will be his alone, so is responsibility for failure.

Hard-nosed Australian, Peter Antonie, lightweight single sculling world champion and Olympic heavyweight double sculls champion, describes the mindset necessary for success in single sculling thus: 'There had to be only one bottom line, the buck stops with me. I had to live and die on the performance that I could or couldn't do'.

Antonie was one of the few scullers or rowers to have made the transition from lightweight to heavyweight. In 1992, he and another former lightweight, Steve Hawkins, won the heavyweight double sculls at the Barcelona Olympics. For Antonie this was the perfect race, 'It is clearly the best race I've ever rowed, it was spot on. We were out of the blocks as fast as we could go. I felt like I was out of the boat watching it from outside'.

For three-time world lightweight single sculls champion, Scotsman Peter Haining, single sculling is about self-expression. 'Sculling is about showing off, expressing yourself. Showing how the constraints and deprivation through the long hours of training can be released through a race. In the race you are like a cork exploding out of a champagne bottle.'

Haining recalls the final of the men's lightweight single sculls at the 1986 World Championships held in the UK. Peter Antonie had opened up a large lead on the defending world champion from Denmark, Bjarne Eltang. However, Antonie had rowed himself almost to a standstill in the last few hundred meters of the race and Eltang was gaining on him with every stroke. Haining was impressed by the tenacity and determination that enabled Antonie to hold off Eltang by the barest of margins to take the world title: 'This race was about an athlete refusing to lose, it was total desperation'.

Haining had his own desperate races. In the 1993 world title he was comfortably leading the final of the men's lightweight single sculls through 1,500m when his blade caught a lane buoy and the boat stopped dead in the water. This allowed Australian Olympic double sculls champion Steve Hawkins, who had returned to lightweight sculling, to burst past him. Haining, however, with an unrelenting 300m sprint rating forty strokes a minute, pulled back the large lead from Hawkins to win the race. Haining described how it was:

> …like watching a movie. I could see myself, as well as the others. I could feel everything but nothing. When I caught the buoy I went straight to my plan B strategy which I had worked on with my coach, Miles Forbes-Thomas. During training, Miles had me doing seven-minute workouts on the leg press machine in the gym. He would suddenly jump on the weights and stop me, 'You've caught a buoy what are you going to do?' When I caught the buoy I had rehearsed the situation over and over – I went ballistic! I had to win; if I did not win I could not afford to keep sculling. I had to justify the faith others had put in me. I went that hard my foot stretcher broke!

Haining has kept the foot stretcher. He also kept the buoy. George Parsonage, one of his previous coaches, retrieved it from the water. He had it mounted in a glass case and presented it to Haining at a rowing dinner.

Sculling can be a body and mind experience. It can provide you with physical and mental challenges. In the single you can be as good as you will let yourself be.

CHAPTER 2
Sculling Fundamentals

BOAT TYPES

There are primarily three types of sculling boat: the single-, double- and quadruple-scull. These are propelled by one, two or four scullers, respectively.

- The single-sculling boat (1×) is approximately 8m in length and has a minimum racing weight of 14kg.

- The double-sculling boat (2×) is approximately 9.9m in length and has a minimum racing weight of 27kg.

- The quadruple-sculling boat (quad or 4×) is approximately 13m in length and has a minimum racing weight of 52kg.

Most racing sculls are coxless, steered by the sculler rather than a coxswain. A single- or

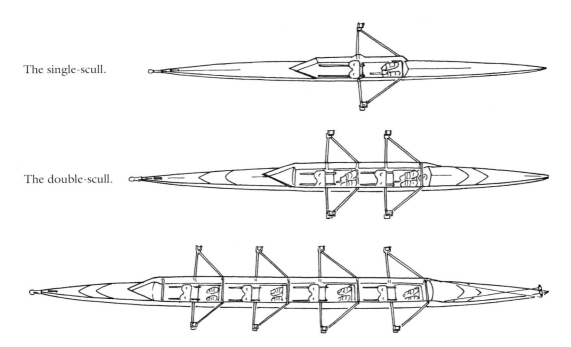

The single-scull.

The double-scull.

The quadruple-scull.

double-sculling boat is steered by either apply-ing more power or sculling for longer on one side than the other. Quadruple-sculls are steered by one of the crew using a rudder on the bottom of the boat.

Coxed quadruple-sculls are used for some school and junior events. Many of the recre-ational boats, which are wider and more stable than their racing cousins, are coxed in order to steer through rivers when touring.

Ocean-racing sculling is the extreme end of the sport. A popular event is the Atlantic Challenge. The trip takes around sixty days and covers approximately 5,400km. The Pacific, of course, takes longer! An ocean-rac-ing single-sculling boat is approximately 7.5m in length, 1.6m in width and has an unloaded weight of 300kg, which increases to approxi-mately 750kg when loaded.

ABOVE: All shapes and sizes can enjoy a sculling outing.

BELOW: An ocean-going double scull.

ROWING CATEGORIES

Sculling is a sport that can be enjoyed simply as a leisure-time activity but it also offers the opportunity to compete at all levels ranging from junior to international and Master categories. International and other major regattas run under the auspices of the International Rowing Federation (FISA) are raced over 2,000m across six lanes. Schools and juniors may have side-by-side regattas that are less than 2,000m. Master's races are organized over 1,000m. Where regattas are held on rivers, the distance and number of crews racing will depend on the particular stretch of water.

Because biomechanical levers and the power of the rower or sculler make a large contribution to performance on water, there is a lightweight category in order to make competitive rowing more widely accessible. The FISA lightweight limits are shown in the table (*below*). Some races may be entered by open-weight and lightweight athletes; others are restricted to the lightweight category. However, lightweight and open-weight sculling and rowing for both men and women are usually available on the same programme.

Lightweights 'weigh in' between 1 and 2h prior to their event. Single lightweight scullers can weigh up to the maximum individual limit. However, when competing in a crew, lightweight scullers have to average their weight out with the other crew members. For example, when competing in the lightweight women's double-scull event, if one crew member weighs 59kg, then the other has to weigh 55kg to achieve the crew average of 57kg. These weight limits may vary at regattas outside of FISA's jurisdiction, such as Henley Royal Regatta and indoor events.

FISA Masters events have eight age categories. These are shown in the table (*above*).

FISA Masters age categories	
Age category	*Age restriction*
A	minimum age 27
B	average age 36
C	average age 43
D	average age 50
E	average age 55
F	average age 60
G	average age 65
H	average age 70

SAFETY

Rowing and sculling are very safe sports, however, being on water and travelling backwards can prove hazardous and the following basic guidelines should be observed.

- You should be able to swim on your front and back, tread water and swim 50m in light clothing.
- If new to the sport, you should be in good health, particularly if you intend to undertake structured and strenuous training sessions. If there is any doubt, consult a medical professional.
- Physically and mentally challenged athletes must always be accompanied.
- Rowing and sculling in the dark is not to be encouraged, however, if it is absolutely necessary, a white light should be shown from the bow and stern.

FISA lightweight limits		
Weight	*Men*	*Women*
	(kg)	*(kg)*
Crew average	70	57
Maximum individual	72	59

Always check local traffic rules and you should boat with your bow into the stream.

A coach or instructor should go through the safety features of the boat before anybody new to rowing or sculling goes afloat on the water for the first time.

- Make sure that the boat has the correct safety features including heel restraints, bow balls and sealed buoyancy tanks.
- Learn the capsize drill and always stay with a capsized boat. You can either swim it to shore or wait for help, using the boat as a giant safety float.
- Learn the water traffic rules before taking to the water. Generally, you will be sitting with your left blade closest to the bank so that traffic coming the other way will pass on the right or stroke side/port side.
- Always check local traffic and boating rules before setting out, particularly on an unfamiliar reach of water. If rowing on tidal stretches of water, be aware of the tidal changes and the strength of the current that comes with incoming and outgoing tides. The best rowing water is generally at the change of tides.

RISK ASSESSMENT

Risk assessment is an important routine that must be undertaken in order to identify

As a new sculler, you will need to practise finding the balance point of the boat before becoming confident in carrying the boat by yourself.

hazards that may affect the safety of the sculling session such as high winds with rough water, fast streams, cold weather, poor visibility, faulty equipment, and lack of appropriate supervision. The level of risk should be assessed and a decision made as to whether or not it is safe to scull. The decision will also be based on an evaluation of the competence and experience of the sculler.

Some agencies and clubs use an effective method based on the traffic-light system to warn of poor water conditions. Green is safe; yellow is a warning and red is danger. If boating alone, these should be strictly observed.

When a situation is being assessed for potential risks, if it looks as if an accident could occur at some stage it is always best to assume that it will and modify the activity accordingly.

CARRYING THE BOAT AND BOATING

To avoid accidents when carrying the boat, it is very important always to be aware of its length and not hit any other boats or the warehouse door! You can balance a single scull on your shoulder and rest the hull against your neck. Holding the rigger to stabilize the boat in one hand, you can carry the sculling blades with the other.

When you reach the dock, squat down and place the blades on the pontoon. Slide the boat off your shoulder and lower it to waist level. You will be holding the rigger on one side and the gunwale on the other.

When putting the boat into the water it is important to reach out far enough to avoid hitting the pontoon with the fin on the bottom of the boat. Once afloat, the sculling blades should be put into the rigger's swivels, first on the pontoon side then the water side of the boat. This will help to keep the boat balanced before stepping into the boat. Hold

Be careful not to drop the sculls as the blades can chip.

Find the edge of the pontoon with your foot so that you do not step into the water.

Always observe good lifting practice by bending from the knees when putting the boat on the water.

both handles for stability; you can then either move from a seated position on the pontoon to sitting in the scull or step on to the footplate and then sit down. You are now ready to scull.

Larger boats are also carried on the shoulders. To float the boat, the crew lower it to waist level and roll it over so it is facing the right way up. One at a time, the members of the crew move around from the water side and hold the boat from the bank side until there is no one left standing between the boat and the water.

As with the single scull, it is important to reach out to avoid the fin or rudder hitting the pontoon when placing the boat on the water. Again, the blades should first be placed in the rigger's swivels that are closest to the pontoon.

ABOVE: When carrying the boat on their shoulders, scullers should pair up with people of a similar height so that the weight of the boat is evenly distributed.

ABOVE RIGHT: To avoid breaking the boat when holding onto internal structures, you should hold onto solid beams and the gunwale, and not the foot stretcher.

RIGHT: Make sure the boat is placed and not dropped on the water. To avoid confusion only one person should be giving orders.

Then, with someone holding the boat, the blades should be placed in the water side swivels and secured. When going afloat in a large boat, half of the crew should hold the boat while the others step on to the footplate and take their seats. They should then hold the boat level and close to the pontoon so the rest of the crew can get in.

THE FIRST STROKES

Before going sculling on the water for the first time, you should have some instruction on the basic sculling stroke. This can be either on a rowing ergometer or in a rowing tank,

I wish I had of been put in a sculling boat when I was thirteen. It would have taught me how to move a boat better. In sculling you can really feel that.

Richard Budgett,
1984 Olympic champion rower

The initial aim should be simply to develop familiarity with the boat and confidence when on the water. Remember that you will not fall in unless you let go of the handles and that as long as you hold the handles at the same height, the boat will remain stable and level. Holding the handles together is called the safety

LEFT: The rowing tank at The Docklands Rowing Centre East London.

BELOW: Level hands mean a level boat.

which is basically a boat-like structure set up in a tank filled with water. Rowing tanks are very good both for teaching beginners and for training in areas that are often affected by extreme weather conditions.

It is good practice and safer for the first few outings in a single sculling boat to take place in calm conditions. Rough or cold water will do little to assist progress or build confidence.

position. If you become nervous or uncertain, you can return to this position and the boat will become level once more.

EXERCISES: CONFIDENCE-BUILDING

The following exercises will help to increase your confidence on the water. It is safer to do these where there is little stream.

1 Make small circles with your hands. First right over left, then left over right—the circles should grow in size until you have the confidence to make very large circles. You can then vary the speed with which you make the circles from very slow to very fast.

2 To demonstrate that quite robust movements are possible without capsizing the boat, try submerging each of the rigger swivels. Put your hands over your knees and

Always start with simple movements and encouragement to build confidence.

The new sculler will be surprised how much the boat can list.

You will learn to feel your balance through your seat.

lift one hand up as high as possible, the other as low as it will go. This will result in the bottom of the rigger swivel going under the water. You should then return to the safety position and submerge the rigger gate on the opposite side of the boat.

3 Once the circles and rigger dipping have been successfully mastered, it is time to try a more difficult exercise. Sitting with your legs flat and the scull's handles close to your body, let go of the handles and raise your hands. The boat may rock around a little at first, depending on your balancing skills, but with practise it should eventually stay level. Grab the handles if you get nervous and fear you may capsize.

4 The last in this series of confidence-building exercises involves standing up in the scull. Put your feet on the footplate in the boat's cockpit. While holding the scull's handles in one hand and holding on to the front arm of the rigger bar with the other, pull yourself up on to your feet. Once standing, there are a variety of exercises you can do such as pointing with one hand and one leg, rowing around in circles each way, and rowing forward in a straight line. The most difficult exercise is to stand up, resting the handle against your shins. Let go of the handle then stand up straight and raise your arms above your head.

TOP: To avoid damaging the boat, make sure you step on the footplate of the boat's cockpit.

ABOVE: Bring the handles together to level the boat.

ABOVE RIGHT: Once the boat is level, hold both handles in one hand.

RIGHT: As your confidence grows, so should the level of difficulty of the exercises.

All these exercises are realistic and will help develop a good level of watermanship. As well as giving you a 'feel' for the boat, they will provide you with the fundamentals necessary for technical improvement.

CAPSIZING

Generally, you will stay in the boat as long as you do not let go of the handles. The sculls provide the stability for the boat. However, there are many reasons why you may capsize. For example, you may 'catch a crab' – this is when the blade of the scull goes into the water at a sharp angle, goes too deep and becomes stuck, which may pull the handle out of your hand. Hitting buoys, debris or other objects on the water can also cause you to let go. Once the grip is lost of one of the handles, you will usually fall in. Although this is not a common occurrence it is very important to learn the capsize drill and to be aware that in the event of capsizing you should stay with the boat as it can be used as a life raft. You can then swim it to shore or wait to be rescued.

EXERCISES: CAPSIZE DRILL

The capsize drill is best done in a swimming pool or in water with little current.

1 Hold on to the front arms of both riggers and roll into the water.
2 Once capsized, pull your feet out of the foot stretcher and swim to one of the riggers.
3 Standing on the rigger, push it under the water while pulling the other rigger towards you to upright the boat.
4 Once the boat is upright, swim to the bow from where it will be possible to swim the boat to shore.

SCULLING AS THE BASIS OF ROWING

Sculling is without doubt the most effective way to learn the skills of watermanship. The single-sculling boat provides you with immediate feedback on your actions. If you are skilful and powerful with good timing, the boat will respond with acceleration and plenty of run. If you are clumsy and cannot time the stroke, the boat will feel heavy and go slowly.

Being on their own, single scullers have no hiding place and have to take and accept responsibility for their performance. This makes the mental demands different from the sweep boats that can share their successes and failures with their crew mates. However, to be successful it is vital that each member takes responsibility for his own performance before looking to the rest of the crew. This attitude can be promoted through training in single-sculls.

Cath Bishop and Katherine Grainger from Great Britain were World Champions in 2003 and silver medallists in the coxless pair at the Athens Olympics. They were also World Cup champions in 2003 and 2004. Six months at the beginning of both seasons were spent sculling with only a minimal amount of sweep rowing. Grainger, who also won a silver medal sculling in the women's quad at the Sydney Olympics, had initial doubts but

OPPOSITE PAGE:
TOP LEFT: You need to roll your weight to the side of the boat that you want to fall over.

TOP RIGHT: You can now use the boat as a float.

MIDDLE: You may need to push your sculls along the side of the boat to be able to pull it over.

BOTTOM: You should always stay with the boat using it as a float. You can either swim the boat to shore or wait for assistance.

Katherine Grainger (left) and Cath Bishop (right) training in Italy prior to their 2003 World Championship victory.

came to appreciate how valuable sculling training was to her rowing.

> We knew that we were going to end up in a sweep boat so at the time it didn't make sense, without doubt. Sculling is challenging, technically, you either move the single or stop it, you learn to become in tune with the water. There is also nowhere to hide; there is always a lot of competition that moves you on. There is no chance to sit back. It is your pride on the line. In sculling you learn a lot about being independent. Sculling develops character and nerve. Once you had done it on your own it seems easier with others. For us, moving back into the pair was a welcome surprise. The winter sculling had put us at a very high standard in the sweep.

In 2005, Grainger stroked the Great Britain quad scull to victory in the World Championships.

Al Morrow is head coach to the Canadian women's team. In addition to many World Championship victories, he led Canada to Olympic success: three golds in Barcelona, another in Atlanta and a bronze in Sydney.

He also believes that training in a single scull is fundamental to competing in every other type of rowing boat. Consequently, sculling plays a major part in his training programme. After victory in the coxless pair and eight in the 1992 Olympics, Marnie McBean and Kathleen Heddle turned to sculling and won another Olympic gold in Atlanta but this time in the double scull. Even while they were still competing in the rowing, much of their training took place in single sculls, which Al believed to be the foundation for every other rowing boat. However, not everyone believed that the transition to sculling would be successful.

> The sculling snobs were saying we will find out how good they really are! Marnie and Kathleen had the basic skills; they had been winning club sculling races since 1988. They had trained a lot in the singles. There is the same mentality in the coxless pair and double scull. Each athlete has to give each other 100 per cent. They were very good at getting a lead around 300m from the start and keeping it.

All rowing programmes would do well to consider the benefits that sculling brings.

CHAPTER 3
Principles of Sculling

Whether you are sculling for recreation or competing at Olympic level, the way the boat moves is the same. It is important to understand the principles that determine the boat's movement, as they will enhance both the speed and efficiency of the boat when correctly applied. These principles relate to the technique the sculler uses, how he rigs his boat and his training, as well as the shape of the boat he chooses to use.

Any object immersed in water is subject to Archimedes' principle, which states that a floating body immerses itself until equilibrium is found between the immersed mass and the displaced water mass. In sculling, the mass refers to the combined mass of the boat and crew. As the mass moves from the catch to the finish position and back to the catch during the stroke cycle, so does the area of maximum displaced water. To stop the boat from having an inefficient rocking movement, boat builders and coaches attempt to spread the displacement over a greater area of the boat. This is achieved through boat length, design and size, as well as the scullers' position in the boat.

It has been stated that up to 88 per cent of the resistance or drag against the water comes from the boat's skin (Herberger *et al.*, 1989). Boat-builders, in an attempt to minimize the drag effect from the water on the boat's hull, have made racing boats proportionally narrower, when compared to their length, than other types of rowing boat. The sculling boat's movement through the water also differs from other boats. While sailing and powerboats can have a constant propulsive force for significant periods, the sculling boat is propelled by the

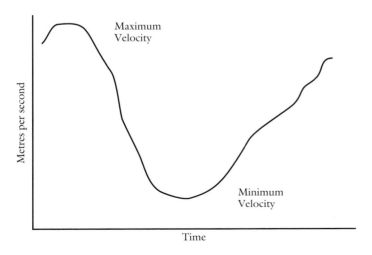

Velocity variation of sculling and rowing boats.

acceleration and deceleration rhythm of the drive/recovery stroke cycle.

Newton's laws of inertia, acceleration, and action determine a boat's velocity. When considering these principles, it is important to understand the following terms:

- **Velocity**: the rate of travel along a chosen route, such as a sculling stroke cycle.
- **Acceleration**: the rate of increase in velocity.
- **Speed**: the distance travelled per unit of time. This differs from acceleration as it occurs irrespective of direction. For example, the speed of John Smith's single scull at rate 18 is 4.36m/s.
- **Power**: this equals force × speed. Power is applied by pulling on the handles of the scull applies force at speed to keep up with the movement of the boat.

Newton's law of inertia states that a body persists in a state of rest or uniform rectilinear movement provided that interacting forces do not alter its state. In sculling, the power phase of the stroke provides the force to push the boat forward. However, drag from the water and environmental conditions can interact against the shell during the stroke and decelerates the boat. Newton's law of acceleration, which states that an increase in velocity is proportional to the acceleration giving force along the line of action (direction) of that force, also applies to this pattern of acceleration/deceleration during the sculling cycle.

Newton's law of acceleration means that when power is applied to the scull's handles and therefore the blades, this provides the impetus and direction to accelerate the boat system forward during the drive phase of the stroke cycle. As the amount of acceleration is proportional to the given force, it is necessary to be able to apply and produce high levels of power.

During the drive and the recovery phase of the stroke, Newton's law of action and reaction applies. This law states that for every action there is an equal and opposite reaction in the opposite direction. During the drive phase, the body mass moves from the catch to the finish of the stroke and, because the blade is connected to the water, the boat is pushed forward. During the recovery, the blades are out of the water and the body mass moving

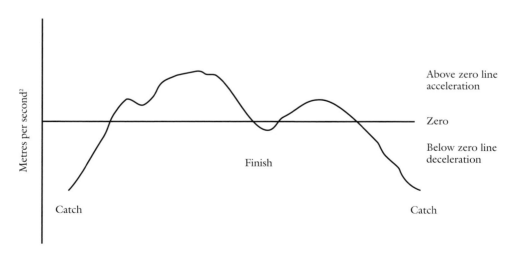

The acceleration/deceleration rhythm of the sculling boat.

from the finish of the stroke to the catch accelerates the boat forward as well. When executed correctly and synchronously, the boat's acceleration is optimized during the recovery phase.

Levers, and the mechanical principles behind them, are fundamental to effective sculling and rigging. The three types of mechanical levers are shown (*right*). The scull moves due to the forces applied through the use of the sculls as levers. The fulcrum (F) is the pivot point of the lever. In sculling this is the pin on the rigger as well as the blade in the water. The effort (E) is the force provided by the sculler, and the resistance (R) is the blades and the boat being moved.

The sculler uses types one and two, of the above lever classes, to propel the boat. As shown, a type one lever has the effort applied at the end of the lever arm with the fulcrum located between the effort and the resistance; these are at either ends of the lever arm. Type two levers still have the effort at the end of the lever arm, however, the fulcrum is at the opposite end of the lever arm with the resistance in between. The type one lever is utilized by the sculler applying power (E) on the end of the scull's handles that levers against the rigger pin (F). The water creates resistance when the blade initially slips in the water at the beginning of the stroke. At this point the pin remains the fulcrum. As the boat moves, the resistance of the water against the blade increases and the blade slippage decreases. This causes the sculling system to become a second-class lever. The effort is applied to the handles, the force and pivot (F) on the blade, and the resistance is the boat being moved past the blades. The effectiveness of the sculling levers is determined by how much skill and power is used to apply the effort.

The effectiveness of the boat's levers will be affected by its gearing. Correct setting of the distance between the fulcrum and resistance

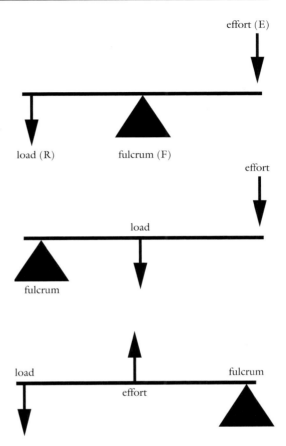

TOP: Class one lever.

MIDDLE: Class two lever.

BOTTOM: Class three lever.

(outboard scull length and span), as well as the distance from the point of work applied (effort) and fulcrum (inboard scull length and span), will ensure that the boat is effectively geared. When selecting the correct gearing, consideration needs to be given to the amount of effort or power you are able to apply. This power can be represented by a force curve, which graphically measures force over sculling angle or stroke duration. It represents the application of power to the lever system, the point during the stroke that maximum power is reached and the total power produced. Each boat class has a different stroke-profile characteristic. With more people, a quadruple-sculling boat goes faster than a double, and a double is faster than a single. The rate of power development required in the early stages of the drive phase of the stroke increases according to the speed of the boat. This is because power has to be applied more rapidly to keep up with the faster boat velocity. The peak force also comes at an angle closer to the start of the stroke. Some people's natural physiological make-up is more explosive than others; these people tend to be suited to the faster boats like the quadruple-scull.

The mechanical laws of sculling also permeate into other areas of the sport. Due to the need for long strokes and levers, most people recruited into sculling are tall and long-limbed, although generally, not as tall as rowers. The symmetrical reach gained in sculling at the front turn is considerably greater than the asymmetrical catch position in rowing. Therefore, shorter people, sometimes overlooked for rowing, may have the opportunity for greater success in sculling.

These mechanical laws are also considered when training on the water, in the gym and on the ergometer. Effective training stroke rates and speeds are calculated from how fast and far the boat travels at a given stroke rate. This is referred to as the boat's distance per stroke and provides the basis for a good sculling rhythm. The boat's rhythm is the ratio between the drive and recovery phases of the stroke cycle. Ergometer training with low rates and low resistance can also promote rhythm and enhance the distance per stroke. Power training in the gym will provide you with the fundamental strength to apply optimum power to the blade. These areas will be covered in greater depth in later chapters.

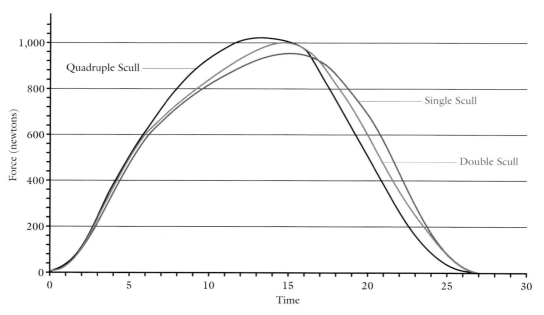

Typical sculling boat force curves.

CHAPTER 4
Sculling Technique

Good sculling technique is based around sound, fundamental, biomechanical principles, the aim of which is to produce an effective and efficient stroke that exploits the mechanical laws governing the propulsion of a sculling boat. The primary influence of the sculler on the boat and its effective movement is called technique. It is important to note the difference between style and technique. Style is an interpretation of particular technical components that the coach or sculler may choose to exaggerate or emphasize. Having a long layback or upright finish position, is an example of style. You will be able to see differences of sculling style in this book, all of which display sound fundamental technical principles. By exploiting mechanical principles and producing a long stroke that achieves both a substantial and efficient distance per stroke as well as high boat-speed, the sculler is able to turn his physical and mental effort into effective and efficient boat speed.

STROKE LENGTH

Correct body sequencing or organization, produces a long stroke that takes advantage of a sculler's natural levers. Long, well-organized strokes start at the finish position of the stroke phase, when the blades are extracted from the water. Immediately after the blades are extracted from the water, the recovery phase takes place. The recovery phase refers to the part of

the stroke cycle when the sculls are out of the water. During this phase, your arms move away from your body at the finish position until your arms are straight, when your body swings over from the hip as illustrated (*below*). As your hands move past your knees and your shoulders swing past your hips, your knees will rise and the seat will travel towards the stern. Flexibility through hips, hamstrings and shoulders will enable you to maximize the length of your levers. Accurate blade work will provide the stroke with effective length by having a longer connection of the scull's blades with the water. The blades will have a minimum amount of 'slip' in the water at their entry and extraction. By the accurate and fast entry of the blades into

The recovery-phase sequence.

the water at the 'catch' position, the boat will maintain a higher minimum speed throughout the 'catch' and drive sequence. This is where the boat speed is at its slowest during the stroke cycle. By maintaining a higher level of minimum boat speed throughout the 'catch' and drive, the average boat speed will be increased.

POWER APPLICATION AND BOAT ACCELERATION

The power application is the effort that is applied to the scull's blades. This power builds and provides the sculling system with inertia. To maximize this power, it is vital to suspend your body weight effectively between the handles and foot stretcher throughout an effectively sequenced drive phase. The power or drive phase, which is initiated with the legs, then trunk, and followed by the shoulders and arms, is the opposite of the recovery sequence. The drive-phase sequence is illustrated (*below*).

RHYTHM

Rhythm is the ratio and relationship between the drive and the recovery phases of the stroke cycle and is the key to effective sculling. All sports have an element of timing: the sweet connection point of a golfer's well-timed swing or a Jonny Wilkinson kick. A good sculling rhythm gives the impression of excessive time during the recovery phase and effortlessness during the drive. When reviewing your technique, always check that the boat is correctly rigged. Many technical faults have their foundation in poor rigging. There are three contact points a sculler has with the boat and the sculls: through the hands, the seat and the feet. The correct position at these points is the basis of executing sound sculling technique.

Position of Hands

Your grip on the scull's handle should be very relaxed. When your arms and hands are tense,

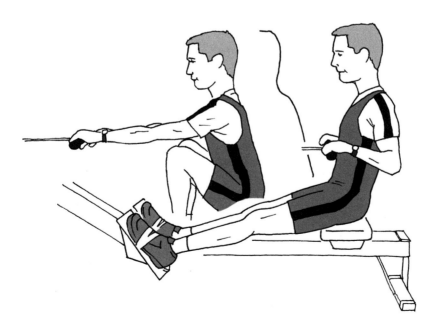

The drive-phase sequence.

Marcel Hacker, former World Champion, Olympic medallist and Diamond Sculls winner, displaying a strong drive grip.

relaxation and, therefore, accurate blade work, are very hard to achieve. Tension creeps down into the arms from the shoulders. This generally occurs because the shoulders are initiating the drive-phase sequence of the stroke instead of the legs. In the drive position of the stroke, the handle should be in the base of your hand. The first set of knuckles (metacarpo-phalangeal joint) should be at 90 degrees, with the thumb on the end of the handle touching the index finger. This position is essential, as the hand-grip has to be as far away from the fulcrum (rigger swivel) as possible. This achieves the most effective effort on the work arm of the lever (inboard length of the scull). It follows a similar principle to that which is used in the opening of a door. The door handle is a long way away from the hinge, thereby maximizing the work arm of its lever.

During the drive phase of the stroke, the wrist is slightly arched to assist with the feathering, or turning, of the sculls after the extraction of the scull's blades from the water. During both the drive and recovery phases of the stroke, lateral pressure should be applied from the thumbs to the end of the scull's han-

dles. This will apply pressure against the rigger swivel. Lateral pressure widens the balance point of the sculler and boat system and, therefore, provides a more stable boat. There is a negative effect on sculling efficiency if lateral pressure is not applied with the thumbs. At the catch position, a lack of lateral pressure will produce a shorter stroke. Moreover, through the finish of the stroke, the scull's collar will lose contact with the rigger swivel and move in and out. This creates an inefficient movement, resulting in a clunking noise at the finish of the stroke.

The position of your forearm is a good reference point to check that you have an effective horizontal drive of the handles. Your forearms should be parallel to the gunwales of the boat throughout the drive, while your grip should stay consistent throughout the drive. As the drive comes to completion with the draw of your arms, you must release the power before the handles reach your body. Once the power is released, your hands, pivoting from the elbow, should apply a downward pressure. This sequence of movements will extract the blade from the water. By a

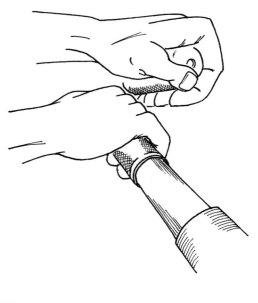

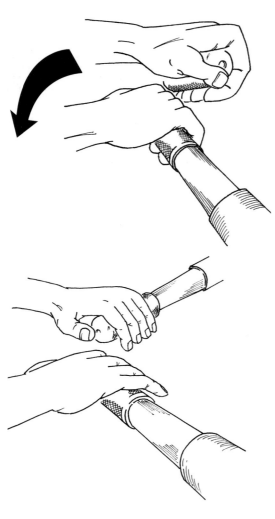

The cross-over.

As your hands move away from your body, your left hand will be very slightly astern, but above, your right hand at the cross-over. This position, which is illustrated (*above*), is recognized almost worldwide as a standard. It is extremely difficult to combine with other scullers in a crew boat if this position is not standard throughout the boat. To achieve this position, the left-hand gate is rigged 1–2cm higher than the right-hand gate.

When your hands are over your ankles, you should start to square the blade to prepare for the entry into the water at the catch position as illustrated (*right*). This is undertaken by a reverse method of feathering: your wrists roll up and your fingers roll down. This action will roll the flat edge of the scull's leather into the flat surface of the swivel gate. As you swing your arms up to place the blades in the water, your grip should be relaxed, so that you can almost feel the handles moving around in your hand.

Feathering the blades.

combination of rolling your fingers and thumb, as well as dropping your wrist, the back of the scull will roll over and thus feather the blade to be parallel with the water as illustrated (*above*). At this point you will have commenced the recovery phase.

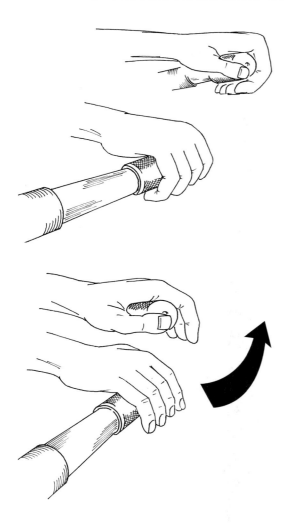

Squaring the blades.

Position of the Seat

The second of the contact points between you and your boat is the seat. A correct sitting position will enable you to achieve an effective body-length position for the catch and, therefore, to undertake an effective drive. This position provides a long stroke and a body position that, with the correct physical conditioning, may reduce the risk of back injury.

When positioned on the seat with your knees down, and in an upright body position, you should feel that you are sitting on the front of your ischial tuberosity, in other words, sitting on the front of the bones of your bottom. You should feel that you could rock over the top of these bones, so as to be on the back of them by the finish position. When you move through to the finish position of the stroke, the seat should be held stable by the activation of the quadricep and gluteal muscles of your legs, as well as the lower abdominal muscles of your trunk. A common error is to overuse the hip flexors, as the lower abdominal and gluteal muscles are commonly weak in scullers and rowers. This can impair the co-ordination and the rhythm of the body during the stroke.

As you move your hands away from your body in the early stages of the recovery, you should feel a stretch throughout the latissimus dorsi muscles, which are found underneath the armpit. You will feel this stretch before your weight shifts on to the front of the bones in your bottom. This will result in the seat slightly moving towards the bow, as your hands and trunk move towards the stern of your boat. When performed correctly, this movement should be made by activating the lower abdominal and gluteal muscles, rather than the hip flexors. Attention should be given in training to developing the lower abdominal and gluteal muscles, so that they have the capacity to achieve this sequence of movements. The development of these muscle groups may assist with injury prevention. Some studies have shown that over-developed hip flexors are frequent causes of lower-back pain.

As your weight shifts from the back of the seat on to the front, it also shifts from your bottom to your feet. If this position, with pelvic tilt, is maintained throughout the recovery, as well as through the catch, positions, a long stroke with an effective connection with the water will be achieved.

Position of Feet

The third and final contact point is your feet. As a proficient sculler, you will be able to feel the run of the boat through your feet during the recovery phase. You will also be able to time, accurately and effectively, your leg drive from the catch position.

When your weight is correctly applied to the foot stretcher, you will feel yourself to be up on top of the boat, rather than down low and inside it. During the recovery phase, you will experience the sensation of the boat coming to you through your feet, rather than your feet pulling you towards the stern. As the seat approaches the end of its rails, your hands must be timed to swing up for the blades to enter the water. Then, with your hands up and the blades buried, you can press through the balls of your feet by activating the gluteal muscles to engage the blades with the water. This commences the drive phase.

In the initial stage of the drive phase, your back should be set in the forward catch position, whilst maintaining your weight on the front of the bones of your ischial tuberosity in your bottom. This position suspends your body weight between the handles and feet, thereby optimizing the effort on the work arm of the sculling lever.

STROKE COMPONENTS

The stroke is divided into four main components: the 'finish', where the blades are extracted from the water; the 'recovery phase', where the blades are out of the water and the boat runs between the strokes; the 'placement', where the blades enter the water; and the 'drive phase', which is the propulsive phase of the stroke cycle.

The Finish

When seated on the back of the ischial tuberosity, the gluteal and quadriceps muscles provide pressure against the foot stretcher. By drawing your hands up, you should be able to feel the blades pushing the water towards the bottom of the river, which will give you the sensation of being light on your seat. As your arms draw the handles into your body, your body should be

Frances Houghton, Olympic silver medallist and World Champion, displaying the correct finish position with level shoulders and hands.

held stable with low and relaxed shoulders. It is important to release the power before the handles are pushed down; this releases the blades from the water. Maintain leg pressure against the foot stretcher throughout the finish sequence. If this is timed correctly, you will have the feeling of constant contact with the foot stretcher throughout the finish and release sequence. Arm speed away from the finish should match handle acceleration of your arms as they come into your body during the drive phase. It is important that your arms are relaxed, so that the handle acceleration developed through the drive is allowed to flow naturally through to the finish position. This will bring your arms forward and shift the weight on to the front of the seat and your feet. When the finish is sequenced correctly, your arms should be straight before your body rocks over from the hips, and your shoulders need to have passed over the front of your hips before your knees rise.

ABOVE: The wrists and fingers are used to feather the blades.

RIGHT: The knees stay flat and the body stable as the arms move away from her body.

Recovery

During the recovery phase of the stroke, you should aim to maximize the distance that the boat travels. This is done by a well-organized body sequence, and by moving in tune with the boat's speed. To achieve a well-organized recovery, your hands need to lead the body sequence from the finish. When your hands lead away from the finish position, and through the cross-over of the handles, it is important that you maintain the handles at the depth that was achieved when you extracted the blades from the water. The path of your hands throughout the finish position is often referred to as the 'shape' of the hands, emphasizing the need for a deep movement; hands should be relaxed throughout this point.

During the recovery phase, the distances travelled by the hands, the body and the legs are different. The hands travel the furthest, followed by the body and then the legs. This is also reflected in the speed each segment must travel to set up and organize the body in preparation for an effective catch position. The recovery sequence has to be hands, body, and then the legs, in order to take advantage of the body's natural levers.

The aim of a well-organized recovery sequence is to achieve full body length and a strong body position by the time you are one-half of the way along the slide. If co-ordination of this movement is well timed, it will increase the boat's acceleration during the recovery. Correct sequencing and timing throughout the recovery also allows for effective and well-timed preparation for the catch.

To maximize the distance the boat travels during the recovery, it is not only necessary to be well-organized with the recovery-body sequencing, but you must also have a 'feel' for the boat's run. This is achieved through shoulder relaxation and feeling for the boat's run through the recovery phase's feet and seat movements. You should be able to feel the boat, or foot stretcher, decelerating towards you at the speed that the boat is decelerating.

Frances displaying a well-organized early recovery. Her hands are over her shins as her knees are lifting and she has maintained good posture and relaxation.

RIGHT: Frances has reached her full body length by the half-slide position.

BELOW: Frances letting her boat run and squaring the blade to place it in the water.

Placement

The end of the recovery phase is the placement of the blade into the water. This is achieved by changing the direction of your hands and the seat at the full-slide catch position, and by commencing the drive phase. The change of direction in the catch position is where there is greatest risk of upsetting the run of the boat and negatively affecting its speed. This phase of the stroke connects the recovery phase with the drive phase. If the blade is buried when your legs commence the drive, there will be a positive effect on the boat's speed. If the drive starts before the placement of the blade, the boat will be kicked backwards with a resulting negative effect on the speed. A sculler with good recovery body sequences and a feel for the boat will be able to change direction more effectively at the catch position. This is the point of the stroke cycle where the boat is moving at its slowest – great accuracy and agility are needed to connect the blade effectively with the water and apply power.

Frances placing the blade in the water as part of her recovery phase.

The Drive

When the placement is timed correctly, you will be able to feel the blades enter and fill with water, and if you are relaxed you will feel your hands move slightly to the stern. Your legs connect, through the balls of the feet, by activating the gluteal muscles. This achieves a suspension between the hands and the feet, with a hanging activation of the latissimus dorsi muscles, which are under the arms.

The drive provides the impulse for the boat's velocity. It is important that power is applied effectively and efficiently, so that the boat can gain and maintain optimal speed. The most effective drive involves the application of legs, body and arms, in a well-timed sequence that makes the boat smoothly accelerate from the catch to the finish. This is the opposite of the recovery sequence. To develop the drive acceleration, the body sequence should be applied from the biggest muscle

groups to the smallest. Therefore, the drive sequence is: legs, body then arms.

This initiation of the drive is called the early drive and is characterized by using your legs to drive the handle and seat back together. The blades should be buried and locked into the water prior to the application of leg power. When this sequence occurs, you are connected and suspended between hands and feet, and you will experience activation of the latissimus dorsi muscles, as well as feeling light on your seat.

Throughout the mid-drive, the body applies its power by swinging back against the driving legs. This provides the handle and, therefore, the blades with horizontal accelerating power. Your arms should be straight with shoulders relaxed and the handles should travel in a flat line.

During the late drive, the legs and body swing are still working together as your arms commence their draw into a stable body at the

The gluteal muscles should initiate the leg drive.

RIGHT: The most effective driving position during the stroke is when the sculls are at 90 degrees to the boat.

BELOW: Frances is displaying a strong grip and arm position.

finish position. When finishing the stroke, draw your arms through with a slightly arched-up wrist, so that the handle can be held high and the blades keep their connection with the water. You will feel your shoulder blades being drawn together. This will put you into a position to be ready to time and execute the extraction of the blade from the water.

BLADE WORK

The aim of good blade work is to maximize the stroke length by efficiently entering and extracting the blade from the water, as well as reducing the blade's wind resistance. The quality of the blade work is determined by the grip, relaxation and stroke sequences.

The timing of the extraction sequence is important for a clean release of the blades from the water. There is a braking effect on the boat's speed if the blades throw up water at their extraction at the finish of the stroke. To avoid this, you should take the power off the handles and then apply downward pressure through your hands to extract the blades from the water. During the drive, the blades develop an air cavity behind them. If you push down quickly, the blades will move cleanly through the cavity without throwing up any water. When the blades are out of the water, you should 'feather' with your fingers, thumbs and wrists. This turning of the blades at 90 degrees reduces the wind resistance against the blades during the recovery. After the blades have been extracted from the water, the puddles behind should form a closed circle, rather than a circle with a tail. If this is the case, they have performed the extraction cleanly.

As the blades are extracted from the water, maintain the height to which your hands are pushed down, as the handles pass over your knees throughout the recovery phase. The blades should travel parallel to the water.

The blades are extracted cleanly from the water.

As the handles separate from their cross-over, squaring of the blades commences with the wrists arching-up, the fingers rolling down

The blades are fully feathered to reduce wind resistance.

and the thumb maintaining lateral pressure. As your hands approach the catch position, your arms and hands lift up and the blades lead down to the water. The blades are then placed in the water as the final part of the recovery phase.

The path of the blades under the water during the drive should be horizontal. Your body weight, moving towards the bow, will cause the bow to push down into the water. Therefore, to keep the blade buried and drawing horizontally, it is necessary to slightly increase the height of the handle throughout the drive.

STROKE CORRECTION

Sculling technique should be a focus of every sculling outing. Perfect sculling practice makes perfect sculling. You need to apply enough concentration to maintain your technical focus for the whole of the outing. A technically good

Accurate blade work produces a longer sculling arc.

sculler will have listened, considered, and taken responsibility for implementing sound technique and the changes required to improve sculling. To achieve a permanent technical change it is important to have a sound understanding of how you are sculling, as well as how you should be sculling. A good coach can impart this knowledge.

When concentrating on stroke correction, you must be able to feel or see a difference in what you are doing and then make the necessary change to your stroke pattern. Video feedback and modelling are excellent aids. The International Rowing Federation produces DVDs of each World Championship and Olympic Games, which provide excellent models of good sculling.

To make a technical improvement, it is often most effective to isolate that part of the stroke that is to be improved. Both the coach and the sculler need to break the complete sculling stroke down into its smaller component parts in order to achieve this. You can correct your stroke by exercises and then by incorporating your improved technical skills into continuous sculling. Major technical improvements generally occur when it is possible to concentrate fully and you are not excessively fatigued. Short sculling, or ergometer sessions, and the beginning of workouts are the best times to achieve stroke correction. This chapter addresses common technical faults and provides sculling exercises to correct them.

POSTURE AND RECOVERY-PHASE BODY SEQUENCING

The over-development of the hip flexor muscles, shortening of hamstring muscles and weak trunk muscles can lead to an ineffective and slumping body position at the catch and finish of the stroke. Stretching of the hip flexors and hamstrings, and trunk strengthening should

take place off the water to correct any imbalances. In the boat, correct body-sequencing will enhance posture, as well as enable you to effectively prepare for the catch and maximize the run of the boat between strokes.

EXERCISES: SLIDE AND BODY LENGTH

This exercise to improve posture and body sequencing has three components: sculling with arms only, sculling with arms and trunk, and sliding to quarter-slide. Isolating the components of the stroke between the finish and the one-quarter slide position will provide an opportunity to concentrate on posture, the recovery sequence and blade work. The correct execution of these positions will create a more efficient boat run and an effective catch position. You will then be in a stronger position to initiate the drive phase.

Twenty to forty strokes in each exercise component should be taken before moving on to the next stage. Once you are proficient with square blades, the level of difficulty may be increased by changing to feathered blades. A further degree of difficulty may then be added by increasing the speed with which you move your hands away from the finish position, while maintaining posture and sequences.

Once you have mastered the exercise as far as the one-quarter slide position, you should move to rolling along the full length of the slide with your seat. You should have finished the body swing by the half-slide position.

ARMS ONLY

The aim of this exercise is to isolate the finish position of the stroke and to practise good posture and arm draw.

Sit in the finish position and activate the gluteal and quadriceps muscles to keep your legs held flat down. The lower abdominal and

Sarah Winckless, bronze medallist from the Athens Olympics and World Champion, demonstrates the arms-only exercise.

back extensor muscles keep the trunk set in a position where the chest is behind the hips. With square blades, take small strokes using only your arms – your body should not move. The handles should move in a rectangular path.

Key points:
- Sit tall and stable in the finish position with your shoulders behind your hips.
- Do not over-extend your shoulders when reaching forward.
- At the handle cross-over, your left hand should be slightly ahead and above your right hand.
- Keep your elbows parallel to the side of the boat.
- Enter the blades into the water as the last part of the recovery phase.
- Ensure that the blades have a consistent shallow depth during the drive phase.

BODY AND ARMS

Once the arms component has been executed proficiently, the trunk can be introduced into the stroke. The aim of this component is to maintain your trunk's posture by the correct muscle activation and sequences during the body swing from the finish of the stroke.

When moving from using arms-only strokes, it is important to keep your legs down by activating the gluteal and quadricep muscles. When your arms straighten, pull in with the lower abdominal muscles. The momentum of the handle and the correct sequencing of muscle activation enables your body to swing over from the hips. This posture should be maintained from the finish to the catch. Good posture will ensure a natural alignment between the lumbar spine and pelvis. There will be neither excessive extension nor flexing through the trunk.

43

The arms and bodies exercise promotes good posture and sequences.

Key points:
- Straighten your arms before your trunk rocks over.
- Use the lower abdominal muscles to draw your tummy towards your spine to rock over.
- Maintain alignment between your lumbar spine and pelvis.
- At the handle cross-over, your left hand should be slightly ahead and above your right hand.
- Enter the blades into the water as part of the recovery of the stroke.
- Maintain a horizontal draw of the handles throughout the drive phase.
- In crewed sculling boats, handle heights and speed should be matched.

ONE-QUARTER SLIDE

The third component of this exercise involves lifting your knees and moving the seat up the slide. The aim is to maximize the body's posi-tion and length in preparation for the catch. Executed in time with the boat's speed, the run of the boat during the recovery phase of the stroke will be maximized.

As you reach your hands towards your ankles and your shoulders pass the seat, relax the gluteal and quadricep muscles. Your knees will rise and the seat will start sliding up the rails. Executed correctly, more of your body weight will be felt in your feet rather than the seat. This means that you will be able to control the boat during the recovery. By maintaining your trunk in this strong posture, you should be almost in the catch position by the time the seat is at the one-quarter slide position.

Key points:
- Maintain the correct arm, body and leg sequence.
- Rock your trunk over from your hips.
- At the handle cross-over, your left hand should be slightly ahead and above your right hand.

Placed correctly during the recovery, Sarah will have a little bit of back splash from her blade.

- Shift weight from the seat to your feet.
- Ensure that the same one-quarter slide point is achieved on the slide of every stroke.
- In a crew sculling boat, all crew members should have identical hand speed and handle height from the finish to the one-quarter slide position.

EXERCISE: PAUSED SCULLING

Paused sculling at the three positions described above is another exercise to improve posture, as well as recovery-phase sequencing and positioning. Similar key points apply to this exercise as for the slide and body-length exercise. Paused sculling should be alternated with continuous sculling. It can be done in blocks of ten strokes followed by twenty normal strokes. This exercise can be done with feathered or square blades.

PAUSE AT ARMS ONLY

The aim of pausing at arms only is to check that you are in the correct finish position. As with arms-only sculling, you should activate the gluteal and quadricep muscles, to keep your legs held flat down. The lower abdominal and back extensor muscles will keep your trunk set in a position where the chest is behind the hips.

Key points:
- Sit tall and stable in the finish position with your shoulders behind your hips.
- Activate the quadricep and gluteal muscles to hold your legs down.
- Do not over-extend your shoulders when reaching forward.
- Keep shoulders low and relaxed.
- At the handle cross-over, your left hand should be slightly ahead and above your right hand.
- Keep elbows parallel to the side of the boat.

45

ABOVE: The arms must stay straight and the body stable.

LEFT: The lumbar spine and pelvis should be aligned in this pause position.

PAUSE AT ARMS AND BODY

Pausing at arms and body is an exaggerated position that ensures the correct sequencing of the transition from the finish to recovery phase of the stroke. The aim of this component of the exercise is to maintain the trunk's posture by the correct muscle activation and sequences during the body swing from the finish of the stroke.

Keep your legs down by activating the gluteal and quadricep muscles. With arms straight, pull in with the lower abdominal muscles. The momentum of the handle and the correct sequencing of muscle activation will enable your body to swing over from the hips. This posture should be maintained. As with arms and body sculling, good posture will lead to a natural alignment between the lumbar spine and pelvis. There will be neither excessive extension nor flexing through the trunk.

Key points:
- Straighten arms before your trunk rocks over.
- Use the lower abdominal muscles to draw your tummy towards your spine to rock over.
- Maintain alignment between lumbar spine and pelvis.
- Do not over-extend your shoulders when reaching forward.
- Keep shoulders low and relaxed.
- At the handle cross-over, your left hand should be slightly ahead and above your right hand.
- In crew sculling boats, handle heights and speed should be matched.

PAUSE AT ONE-QUARTER SLIDE

The aim of pausing at the one-quarter slide position is to maximize the body's position in preparation for the catch. Executed in time with the boat's speed, the run of the boat will be maximized during the recovery phase of the stroke.

As you reach with your hands towards your ankles, and your shoulders pass the seat, relax the gluteal and quadriceps muscles. Your knees will rise and the seat will start sliding up the rails. Executed correctly, more of your body weight should be felt in your feet rather than the seat, which will help you to control the boat during the recovery. By maintaining your trunk in this strong posture, you should be almost in the catch position by the time the seat is at the one-quarter slide position.

Key points:
- Maintain the correct arm, body and leg sequence.
- Rock trunk over from your hips.
- At the handle cross-over, your left hand should be slightly ahead and above your right hand.
- Shift weight from the seat to your feet.
- The same one-quarter slide point should be achieved on the slide of every stroke.
- Keep shoulders low and relaxed.
- In a crew sculling boat, all crew members should have identical hand speed and handle height from the finish to the one-quarter slide position.

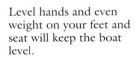

Level hands and even weight on your feet and seat will keep the boat level.

EXERCISE: POSTURE AND DRIVE-PHASE BODY SEQUENCING

The most difficult part of the stroke to synchronize is the placement of the blades in the water at the catch and applying leg power. At this point of the stroke cycle, the boat is moving at its slowest and the body mass of the sculler or crew has its greatest opportunity to work against the positive run of the boat. To maximize the boat's run, the blades should be buried before applying power to the drive phase of the stroke. If this change of direction from the recovery phase to drive phase is well timed, the effective length is increased and more power can be applied, making it possible to push the boat further with every stroke. Your position during the recovery will determine how effective the change of direction will be at the catch position. Your trunk should be at full length by the half-slide position. You should be relaxed and feel your body weight through your feet as the seat rolls along the slide. Swing your arms up to bury the blade, as the seat rolls to the end of the slide. As the blades are buried and grip or pick up the water, activate the gluteal muscles in the buttocks, applying power through your legs – this commences the drive phase. Power should then be applied through the legs, trunk and arms – the reverse body sequence to that used in the recovery phase.

As with the recovery phase, the drive phase can be reduced to its component parts, corrected and then re-introduced into the full sculling strokes.

EXERCISE: FRONT TURN AND DRIVE

The front turn and drive exercise can achieve drive-phase correction. It is divided into three components: legs only; legs and body; and legs, body and arms. It is best executed at 75 per cent pressure.

LEGS ONLY

In this exercise it is necessary to have good posture when you are coming in and out of the front turn. Start by sitting at the half-slide position with good posture and in the catch position. Roll along the slide, placing the blade in the water and activate the gluteal muscles to apply leg power. Maintain your trunk in the strong catch position. Initially the legs should only be driven down one-quarter of the way. As you feel the 'pick up' and application of power, the leg drive should get longer until you are using the first half of the slide. Executed correctly, you will be suspended between your hands and feet and feel very light on your seat.

Key points:
- Maintain good posture so that the trunk position is maintained throughout the exercise.
- Enter the blades into the water before applying leg power.
- The initial leg drive is applied by the gluteal muscles.
- There is suspension between the hands and feet.
- Maintain stroke length.

LEGS AND BODY

This component of the exercise concentrates on the power provided by the trunk during the drive phase of the stroke. Connect in the same way as you would for the legs-only component of the exercise. After the first one-quarter of the drive, engage your hips, abdominal muscles and lower back in order to open your trunk against your legs to add more power to the middle of the stroke. Finish the stroke without using your arms. If you can feel the suspension between your feet and hands lasting longer through the drive, you are well-connected and applying effective power.

The aim of this exercise is to make your leg drive more effective.

You will feel a strong connection between your legs and back.

Once rowing with all the drive components, you should feel well-connected powerful strokes.

Key points:
- Maintain good posture, so that the trunk position is maintained throughout the exercise.
- Enter the blades into the water before applying leg power.
- The initial leg drive is applied by the gluteal muscles.
- Maintain your trunk in the catch position for the first one-quarter of the drive.
- There is suspension between the hands and feet for the whole of the drive.
- Shoulders should be held low.
- Maintain stroke length.

LEGS, BODY AND ARMS

The shoulders and arms are introduced to finish the drive sequence of the stroke. As your trunk passes over the seat, activate your shoulders to commence the arm draw; this should be a smooth transition during the drive phase. Aim to maintain the level of power on the blades, which has been generated by your legs and trunk, with your shoulders and arms.

Key points:
- Maintain good posture, so that the trunk position is maintained throughout the exercise.
- Enter the blades into the water before applying leg power.
- The initial leg drive is applied by the gluteal muscles.
- Maintain your trunk in the catch position for the first one-quarter of the drive.
- There is suspension between hands and feet for the whole of the drive.
- Shoulders should be held low.
- Initiate arm draw as the trunk swing ceases.

- Hold arms straight until trunk swing has almost ceased.
- Maintain stroke length.

EXERCISE: BALANCE, BLADE WORK AND TIMING

A stable boat allows you to implement and time your stroke effectively. During the drive phase, the boat is held level by the handles of the sculls being drawn through the drive at an even height. Balance during the recovery phase of the stroke is more complicated. It relies not only on holding your hands level, but also on maintaining balance on your feet and seat.

THE ROLL-UP

This is one of the most effective exercises for stroke correction. Executed correctly, it provides a good tool to improve all facets of the sculling stroke.

Sit in the finish position with your knees held down firmly and the blades square in the water. Tap the handles down and, lifting the blade from the water, execute the recovery-phase sequence and drop the blades into the water at the catch position.

As this exercise starts from a stationary boat, you will not benefit from the stability that the momentum of a moving boat provides. To achieve a level boat, you must correctly and definitively execute the correct recovery-phase sequences and handle heights.

There are numerous variations and progressions to this exercise. You can start by rolling out to either the one-quarter or half-slide position to check correct body positioning at those two reference points. Once you are proficient at the roll-up and placement of the blade in the water, you can progress to rolling-up and taking a stroke. To complete the cycle, finish the stroke at the one-quarter slide position with a level boat. Pay particular attention to the stern at the catch. If pressure is applied evenly and correctly, it will move smoothly and evenly through the water. If not, it will fishtail and it will be necessary to check the stroke timing and pressure, in order to adjust the run of the boat. If the blade is correctly placed in the water before applying leg power, the boat will move directly forward. If leg power is applied too early, the stern will kick back before moving forward. As this is a very inefficient way to take the catch, it is important to persevere with the exercise until the stern can evenly and effectively move away from the catch position. Once you are proficient at one stroke, you should move to multiple strokes. As the boat moves faster with each stroke, you will have to execute your skills more quickly and more skilfully.

You can also concentrate on blade-work correction during the roll-ups. Initially, the roll-up can be done with square blades before progressing to feathering. Delayed feather, and early and late squaring, will promote hand skills and improve blade work.

Key points:
- Maintain the correct recovery body sequence: hands, trunk, legs.
- Execute the correct blade work:
  - square and clean release of the blades from the water;
  - early squaring of the blade;
  - blade placement in the water at the catch position as the last movement of the recovery.
- Employ the correct drive sequences:
  - blade placement before leg drive commences;
  - leg drive starts by activating the gluteal muscles in the buttocks; connection and suspension between the buried blades and the feet should be felt;
  - sequence is applied in the reverse order of the recovery sequence: legs, trunk, arms.

51

OPPOSITE PAGE:
TOP: Sit relaxed in the finish position with your hands level. If you force the balance, the boat will crash over to one side when the blades are extracted from the water.

MIDDLE: You need to have your weight on your feet during the recovery to get a 'feel' for the boat on the water.

BOTTOM LEFT: Maintain level handle heights for the boat to stay balanced.

BOTTOM RIGHT: Place the blades in the water as the last thing during the recovery phase.

EXERCISE: BLADE WORK

Poor blade work and tension through the upper body often stems from problems with the grip. Old-timers suggest that holding the handles of the sculls should be like holding a bird – a strong enough grip to hold the bird still but not hard enough to harm it!

Good blade work will provide a stable scull and effective length. A correct grip will ensure correct blade work and add relaxation to the stroke. The following exercises will help in improving grip and blade work. They should be done in twenty-stroke blocks alternating with normal sculling.

OPEN-PALM SCULLING

Open-palm sculling is done at full slide. Once the blade has been squarely extracted from the water and feathered, open your fingers and rest the handle under your first set of knuckles. Concentrate on relaxing your forearms and shoulders, while sliding during the recovery. As the handles pass over your toes, put your fingers back over the handle and square the blade to take the catch of the next stroke.

Key points:
• Keep thumbs on the end of the handles.
• Relax arms and shoulders.
• Keep wrist flat with your palm open.
• At the cross-over, your right hand is close to, and under, your left hand.

Open-palm sculling promotes relaxation through your arms and shoulders.

SQUARE BLADES

This is one of the most popular exercises in rowing and sculling. The blades are left square for the whole of the stroke, which forces you to find enough blade height off the water to execute the recovery without the blades hitting the water. When you return to feathering the blades, you should keep your hands on the same path.

Key points:
- Hold wrists flat throughout the stroke.
- Extract blades cleanly and squarely at the finish of the stroke.
- At the cross-over, your right hand is close to, and under, your left hand.
- Blades should be fully square, not half-squared or half-feathered.
- Hold blades evenly off the water on both sides of the boat.

BELOW: Keep hands in the drive-grip position.

DOUBLE SQUARE

This exercise, which is a progression from the delayed feather, requires you to feather and square the blades twice in one recovery phase. It promotes dexterity in the hands, as well as relaxation during the recovery. Grip and shoulders must be extremely relaxed, so that the blade can come back fully on to the feather and then back fully on to the square, before having to take the catch. This exercise also assists in the correction of the blade height during the recovery. The handle height has to be consistent as you square and feather.

Key points:
- Employ a relaxed grip.
- Maintain consistent handle height.
- At the cross-over, your right hand is close to, and under, your left hand.
- Blades are either on the square or feathered, not somewhere in between.
- Square blades at the same time on both sides of the boat.

CHAPTER 5
Rigging

Correct rigging and gearing are essential in sculling. Rigging refers to the adjustments that can be made to the boat and blades to make the sculler more effective. This includes the height of the rigger and feet, the position of the sculler in the boat, and the angle that the oar is set to come through the water. Gearing refers to the adjustment of the boat's levers to achieve the optimal loading during racing and training conditions.

The rigging and gearing of a boat can be individualized to provide the set-up best suited to the sculler's physical dimensions. Poor rigging can often cause technique problems. Coaches should regularly check that the boat is rigged correctly in order to be confident that it is the sculler who needs to be improved, not the boat's rigging! Rigging and gearing can also be used to combine members of a crew, irrespective of their size and skills, to make the

boat's rig effective and comfortable for each individual.

The fundamental rigging points that will be referred to throughout this chapter are illustrated (*below*).

- **Span**: the distance between the centre of the rigger pin on the bow side (left) and the centre of the rigger pin on the stroke side (right).
- **Sill to seat height (height 1)**: the height measured from the lowest point on the seat to mid-point on the sill of the rigger swivel.
- **Seat to feet height (height 2)**: the height measured from the lowest point on the seat to the lowest point inside the heel of the shoe on the foot stretcher.
- **Deck to water height (height 3)**: the height measured from the deck of the boat to the water surface.

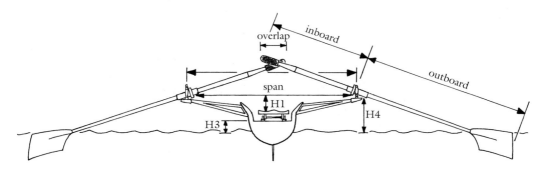

Key rigging points.

- **Sill to water height (height 4)**: the height measured from the midpoint on the sill of the rigger swivel.
- **Inboard**: the distance from the tip of the handle to the outboard side of the collar of the scull.
- **Outboard**: the outboard is the distance from the outboard side of the collar to the point on the end of the blade that is a continuation of the line created by the shaft.
- **Overlap**: the distance that both handles overlap each other (the length of the inboard and the span determines this distance).

The aim of gearing the boat is to enable you to maintain your rate, race and stroke profile for the duration of the event. Scullers and crews who are geared too hard tend to start their races fast, rate low and become slower over the length of the course. Those geared too lightly tend to rate very high but do not keep up with their lower-rating competitors. Correct gearing will produce a stroke rate profile and rhythm that can be maintained for the duration of the race.

Strong wind and water conditions affect the overall time of a race, which will be shortened by a tailwind and lengthened by a headwind. This, in effect, changes the gearing. To assist in overcoming extreme conditions, the gearing can be eased or hardened by changing the foot-stretcher position, adjusting the span or adjusting the length of the outboard of the sculls.

Moving the foot stretcher towards the stern of the boat will make the gearing harder. During the drive phase, the direction of force applied from the blade to the water changes in direction. Predominately, the direction of force always follows the angle of the blade in the water. At the catch, the direction is away from the boat. As the scull's blades move past 90 degrees to the rigger swivel, the force is pushing in the opposite direction to which the boat is travelling. During the final-third of the drive, the force is directed in towards the boat. The optimal drive position for the blade is at 90 degrees to the rigger's swivels. This line between the swivels is referred to as 'square-off'. The direction of the blade force during the drive phase is illustrated (*below*).

When the foot stretcher is set forward towards the stern of the boat, the angle at the catch becomes greater. Consequently, the force created by the stroke will be directed laterally away from the boat, and the blade will have longer in the water to apply power. This approach is used in a race situation with a considerable tailwind, where the time of the race will be shortened due to the wind. By hardening the gearing, you can apply power over a longer period. This method of changing gearing is also the most effective in variable conditions, as it offers the possibility of changing the gearing right up to the start of a race. An alternative is to insert a 'clam' plate on to the shaft of the oar between the collar

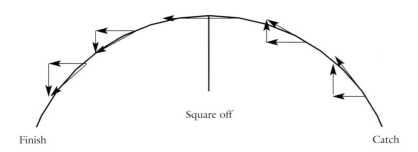

Square off

Finish

Catch

Blade-force direction during the drive phase.

and the swivel. If conditions change, the 'clam' can be removed to change the gearing. All other methods have to be done on the land. The term 'work through' describes the distance from square-off to the point on the slide reached in the catch position. This measurement should be recorded. Through trial and error, you can set the best catch position for all types of conditions.

Changing the span also adjusts the gearing when wind conditions are extreme. If the scull length stays the same and the span decreases, there is a longer arc in the water. This results in the blade being in the water longer and therefore hardening the gearing. In tailwind conditions it is advantageous to gear the boat to the conditions. Conversely, by making the span wider and maintaining the scull length, the gearing is lighter. The oars will be in the water for a shorter time and therefore best suited to strong headwind conditions.

Changing the outboard length of the scull is the most popular way of adjusting the gearing. It is also the simplest and most time-efficient method. Adjusting the collar position on the scull will achieve a gearing change. Following the same principles as with the span, the outboard length of the scull can be increased by moving the collar closer to the handle. This provides a longer arc and therefore more time with the blade in the water to apply power for the tailwind condition. Alternatively, placing the collar closer to the blade decreases the outboard and gearing, which is an adjustment made for a headwind. If using adjustable sculls, you will also be able to change the total scull length, which will increase the gearing. Again, through trial and error, you will find which method works best for you.

When setting gearing, consideration needs to be taken of your height and fitness level, together with the event's duration. Your height will determine the length of the arc that you row. Taller and fitter scullers should take advantage of their long limbs and power by setting up to scull with a long arc; this will make gearing quite hard. They will tend to rate lower with a long arc and to move their boat further each stroke, thereby taking fewer strokes to complete the distance. This makes the gearing more physically efficient for the taller, stronger sculler.

Smaller or weaker scullers will not be able to maintain technical form with such a heavily geared boat and must consider the effect of the physical exertion of each stroke against the number of strokes they must produce. To achieve the optimal balance between the distance per stroke and the number of strokes, they generally use an easier gearing. This results in a lighter load but a higher rate of strokes per minute. However, when preparing for long head races that can take up to 20min, then, like taller scullers, they should consider a harder gearing than for a 2,000m race. This will again create a longer arc and a lower rate of stroking. Due to the long duration of a head race it is important not to expend too much energy taking too many strokes.

Optimal gearing is achieved through trial and error during training. To assess and measure the effectiveness of the gearing, a gearing ratio is used. The following equation calculates the standard accepted gearing ratio, which is used for each rigger's gearing. Therefore, the ratio is for one side of the boat. The effective outboard of the scull is divided by the rigger's span. To do this the hypothetical centre of blade pressure must be used. Although there are many blade shapes, 12cm inside from the blade's tip is the hypothetical centre of pressure.

$$\frac{(\text{length of scull} - \text{inboard} - 12)}{(\text{half the scull's span})}$$

For example, if you are rigged with a 159cm span, in a scull with a length of 290cm with

88cm inboard, you will calculate your gearing ratio as follows:

$$\frac{(290 - 88 - 12)}{(159/2)} = \frac{190}{79.5} = 2.390$$

The higher the ratio figure, the harder the gearing.

To have a comfortable and effectively rigged boat, the following adjustable positions need to be considered:

- rigger swivel sill to seat height;
- seat to foot height;
- deck to water height;
- rigger swivel sill to water height.

The rigger swivel sill to seat height is a major contributor to a sculler's comfort. It can affect

the stroke's length and can lead to technical faults, including incorrect blade height and boat instability. This is one of the few rigging adjustments that are not symmetrical between the left and right sides of the boat. As the sculler uses two oars, there is a cross-over of the handles during the drive and recovery phases of the stroke. To stop the handles hitting each other, one hand has to travel ahead or below the other. For crew sculling boats, the accepted practice is that the left hand should be above and slightly ahead of the right. This provides enough overlap without affecting the balance and provides enough symmetry between both arms to maintain even stroke length on both sides of the boat. This standard practice is especially important when combining scullers in a crew. Balance and consistent stroke length would be difficult without it. Different overlap hand positions in

Recommended rigging/gearing tables for men's sculling boats

Boat type	Span (cm)	Scull length (cm)	Inboard (cm)	Gearing ratio
Senior single (1×)	159	291	88	2.403
Junior/club single (1×)	159	290	88	2.390
Senior double (2×)	159	292	88	2.415
Junior/club double (2×)	159	291	88	2.403
Senior quad (4×)	158	292	87	2.443
Junior/club quad (4×)	158	291	87	2.430

Recommended rigging/gearing tables for women's sculling boats

Boat type	Span (cm)	Scull length (cm)	Inboard (cm)	Gearing ratio
Senior single (1×)	160	288	88	2.350
Junior/club single (1×)	160	287	88	2.338
Senior double (2×)	159	289	88	2.377
Junior/club double (2×)	159	288	88	2.365
Senior quad (4×)	158	290	87	2.418
Junior/club quad (4×)	158	289	87	2.405

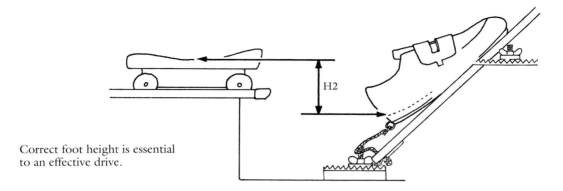

Correct foot height is essential
to an effective drive.

the same sculling crew will adversely affect the boat's rhythm and the comfort of the crew. To achieve this cross-over height differential, the left rigger swivel sill should be rigged 1–2cm higher than the right.

The rigger swivel sill to seat height is generally 16–19cm, depending on the weight, thigh thickness and height of the crew. The taller and heavier the crew, the greater the height required.

The seat to feet height and foot-stretcher angle will determine how effective the leg drive will be through the stroke. This is also influenced by how effectively you can get

your body weight on to the foot stretcher during the recovery phase of the stroke. If done correctly, it will help you to control the run and balance of the boat. If you have long shins and legs, your feet will be set deeper into the boat. As a result, your knees should be just below your arms when you are compressed in the catch position of the stroke. The range of this measurement is generally 16–19cm for women and 18–22cm for men.

The rake of the foot stretcher should be 42 degrees +/– 3 degrees. For scullers with poor ankle flexibility, the rake of the foot stretcher can be adjusted (flattened), so that they can get

Feet too high and steep.

comfortably into the compressed catch position of the stroke. If the rake is too steep and the height too high, the drive-phase pattern will be affected as illustrated (*see* p.59). The tendency is to over-use the trunk at the expense of the leg drive, producing an ineffective drive pattern. If the rake and foot height is too shallow, the legs will have an ineffective drive pattern. The trunk

Feet too low and shallow.

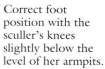

Correct foot position with the sculler's knees slightly below the level of her armpits.

will again dominate the legs as illustrated (*top left*). When the foot height and rake are correctly adjusted as illustrated (*bottom left*), the drive phase will be horizontal with the trunk, working effectively against the legs. When adjusted correctly, the knee should be slightly below the armpit in the catch position.

The deck to water height is determined by the size of the boat, and is set at the point of boat manufacture. If the boat is correctly sized for the crew, they will feel comfortably on top of the water with the manufacturer's standard seats. If the boat is too low with the deck to water height, you will experience an uncomfortable feeling of sitting too deep in the boat. This is why it is important to purchase a boat in the correct weight range. The seat may be vertically adjusted to compensate, although there is a limit to how much the seat can be adjusted.

The rigger swivel sill to water height is also measured when you are sitting in the boat and the water is calm. The greater the rigger swivel sill to water height, the steeper the angle of the scull shaft from the hand to the water. When at the compressed catch position, the angle of the scull shaft is called the angle of attack. If the angle is too shallow, the stroke becomes too short; if the angle is too steep, the blade will dig too deep, producing an ineffective path of the blade in the water.

The rigger gate sill to water height is generally 26–28cm.

RIGGING THE SCULL

Due to the size of a scull, it is very difficult to rig a boat on your own. For greater accuracy, rigging should be done with two people. For consistency, the same person should undertake the same measurement tasks on both sides of the boat.

Initially, the boat's riggers are fixed to the boat with enough adjustment to give the appropriate sill to seat height range. The swivels should be stripped down to the pin. Using a quality builder's spirit level, the boat is set level in both length and width. The boat should be clamped level to upright posts, so that measurements and adjustments can be made without disturbing the level platform of the boat.

The span is measured from the middle of the base of the right-hand-side rigger pin to the middle of the base of the left-hand-side rigger pin with a tape measure. It is important to measure at the base of the pin; if there is a lateral lean on the pin, the measurement will not reflect the true span. Once the correct span is achieved across the boat, the pins are adjusted to be identical distances from the midline of the boat. Boat-builders set the seat rails in the centre of the boat. Measure from the opposite rail to the closest edge of the base of the rigger pin on either side of the boat. If there is a difference in these measurements, adjust until they are the same on either side of the boat, whilst maintaining the

Recommended height levels				
	Men (cm)	Lightweight men (cm)	Women (cm)	Lightweight women (cm)
Sill to seat	17–19	16–18	16–18	15–17
Seat to feet	18–22	16–19	16–19	16–18
Sill to water	26–28	26–28	26–28	26–28

required span. If the rigger pins are unequally set, the gearing will be different between the left- and right-hand sides of the boat, and you will have difficulty steering.

Once the span is correct, the 'pitch' should be set. The pitch refers to the vertical angle that the blade is set at in the water. Determining the pitch is the angle of the rigger swivel and the angle set on the sleeve of the scull. To set the rigger swivel's pitch, the rigger pins should be checked with spirit levels or pitch gauges, and adjusted until they are vertical longitudinally, as well as laterally. The boat must be held level for accurate measurement. Pitching inserts in the swivels adjust the pitch of the gate. Trial and error needs to be used to select the correct pitch to suit individual technical abilities. Nonetheless, 5 degrees is a good starting point. When selecting the pitch to use, it is important to know whether there is any pitch on the scull's sleeve. Most sculls come with 0 degrees from the manufacturer. However, if the scull has pitch, the number of degrees has to be added to the swivel pitch to provide the true pitch.

Once the span and pitch are correctly adjusted, the sill to seat height can be measured. There are a number of height-measuring tools available. These range from a straight-edged piece of timber, through to laser-based precision tools. The most effective and cost-efficient tool is an adjustable telescopic height stick available from leading boat-builders and suppliers. A measurement is made from the mid-point of the rigger swivel sill to the boat's deck at a point 90 degrees to the face of the rigger swivel. A measurement from the same point of the deck to the lowest point of the seat is then made. The sill to seat height equals the seat to deck measurement subtracted from the deck to sill height.

To measure the seat to feet height, a long straight edge is required. The straight edge is placed across the gunwale of the boat over the seat at a point 90 degrees from the face of the rigger swivel. The seat to feet height equals the distance from the seat to the gunwale subtracted from the distance at the lowest point inside the heels of the foot stretchers to the gunwale. Once the seat to foot height is set,

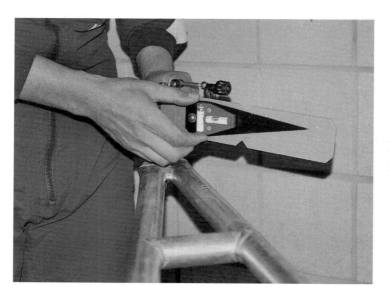

A pitch meter is an effective tool to measure a boat's pitch.

ABOVE: Make certain the height is measured to the same point on the swivel every time you measure.

RIGHT: A steel rule is a most effective tool to measure the seat height.

the rake of the foot stretcher can now be adjusted.

Most scullers row with their sculls at approximately 40 degrees at the finish of the stroke and 60 degrees at the catch. Using trigonometry, angles from the midline of the boat, and the boat's span, can accurately position the foot stretcher.

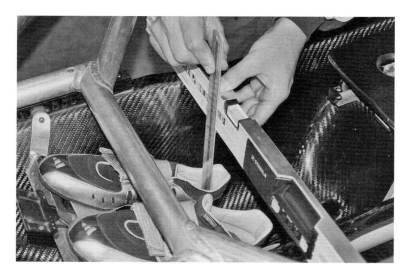

LEFT: Make sure the end of the steel rule is at the lowest point of the shoe's heel.

BELOW: Always measure with the seat at the same slide position. Due to the gradient of the slide, a false reading will be given unless the seat is in the same position each time it is measured.

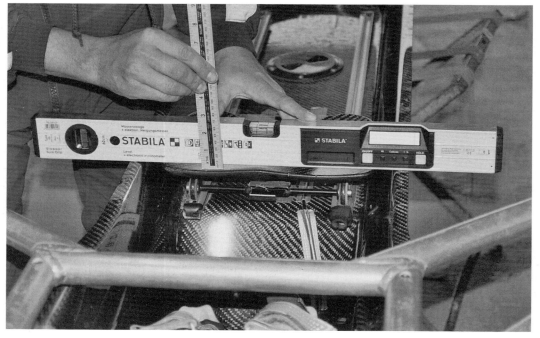

A guide to position the feet									
Catch angle					Span (cm)				
	157.0	157.5	158.0	158.5	159.0	159.5	160.0	160.5	161.0	161.5
65	185.7	186.3	186.9	187.5	188.1	188.7	189.3	189.9	190.5	191.1
64	179.1	179.6	180.2	180.8	181.4	181.9	182.5	183.1	183.6	184.2
63	172.9	173.5	174.0	174.6	175.1	175.7	176.2	176.8	177.3	177.9
62	167.2	167.7	168.3	168.8	169.3	169.9	170.4	170.9	171.5	172.0
61	161.9	162.4	163.0	163.5	164.0	164.5	165.0	165.5	166.0	166.6
60	157.0	157.5	158.0	158.5	159.0	159.5	160.0	160.5	161.0	161.5
59	152.4	152.9	153.4	153.9	154.4	154.8	155.3	155.8	156.3	156.8
Finish angle					Span (cm)				
	157.0	157.5	158.0	158.5	159.0	159.5	160.0	160.5	161.0	161.5
45	111.0	111.4	111.7	112.1	112.4	112.8	113.1	113.5	113.8	114.2
44	109.1	109.5	109.8	110.2	110.5	110.9	111.2	111.6	111.9	112.3
43	107.3	107.7	108.0	108.4	108.7	109.0	109.4	109.7	110.1	110.4
42	105.6	106.0	106.3	106.6	107.0	107.3	107.7	108.0	108.3	108.7
41	104.0	104.3	104.7	105.0	105.3	105.7	106.0	106.3	106.7	107.0
40	102.5	102.8	103.1	103.5	103.8	104.1	104.4	104.8	105.1	105.4
39	101.0	101.3	101.7	102.0	102.3	102.6	102.9	103.3	103.6	103.9
38	99.6	99.9	100.3	100.6	100.9	101.2	101.5	101.8	102.2	102.5
37	98.3	98.6	98.9	99.2	99.5	99.9	100.2	100.5	100.8	101.1
36	97.0	97.3	97.6	98.0	98.3	98.6	98.9	99.2	99.5	99.8
35	95.8	96.1	96.4	96.7	97.1	97.4	97.7	98.0	98.3	98.6

To use this table, a string line needs to be set from the boat's bow ball to the tip of the boat's stern. It is best to tie the string line around the bow ball and, using adhesive tape, adhere it to the middle of the stern canvas. With a tape-measure, and another piece of adhesive tape, set the string line to the midline of the boat.

For example, you are to be set at 40 degrees in the finish position with a span of 159cm. A tape-measure is required to measure the point on the string line 103.8cm from the middle of the face of the gate. Mark this 40-degree point on the boat with a marker pen. When you are sitting in the boat, you need to adjust the foot stretcher, so that when you are at the finish position, the back edge of the shaft of the scull is over the top of the 40-degree mark. Once your feet are set, the seat's rails should be adjusted so that you will almost touch the front stops in the compressed catch position.

Sculling boats have from one to four crew members. The different sculling-boat classes each display different power profiles. The bigger and faster the boat, the earlier that power is applied during the stroke. This is because power has to be applied more quickly to keep up with

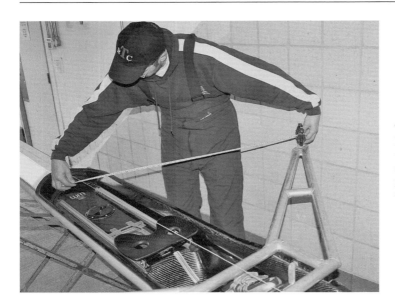

Thames Rowing Club High Performance Club Coach, Gary Stubbs, measuring the finish position on a single scull.

the speed of the fast boat. Generally, this means that quads are rigged further towards the stern than doubles, and doubles are rigged further towards the stern than singles.

Measuring the water to sill height needs to be done while you are in the boat and on the water. The level of the boat needs to be held laterally with the aid of a spirit level. The distance is measured, with a tape-measure, from the middle of the rigger swivel sill to the water. The sill to water height can be changed through the adjustment holes on the rigger arms or through the washers under the rigger swivel pin.

All nuts and bolts should be checked to ensure that they are tight but not over-tightened. The back arm, if used, should be loosened and tightened in the following order. First, those nuts tightening the back arm to the rigger, and then those tightening the pin and, finally, the clips that hold the two sections of the back arm together.

Once the boat has been rowed, you should determine whether the sculler is comfortable, and that the rig is correct.

INDIVIDUALIZED RIGGING IN CREWED SCULLING BOATS

Rigging double- and quadruple-sculling boats follows the same process for each seat as is done for a single-sculling boat. However, rigging may be individualized within the crew boat. This increases the gearing effectiveness and the comfort of the crew. The most common form of individualizing a crewed boat is to adjust the span to bring the arcs of a sculling crew uniformly together. Extremely tall scullers, with a naturally long reach, can have their span and outboard extended to reduce their arc, bringing the crew's angles together. Conversely, shorter scullers may be lengthened by reducing the span and outboard on the sculls, increasing their sculling angles to that of the rest of the crew.

Once the boat is correctly set up, the focus can then be confidently turned to improving the technical and mental skills as well as physical conditioning.

CHAPTER 6
Physiological Requirements of Sculling

Effective rowing and sculling requires the athlete to display flexibility, an ability to produce power, balanced musculature and a strong aerobic capacity. Whether competing in 2,000m competitions, 1,000m Master's races, long head races or recreational rowing and tours, you will benefit from addressing these areas in your training. It is important to have an understanding of the fundamental principles of the physiological requirements of sculling events, so that you can undertake the most effective training to improve your performance. This chapter provides an overview of some of these physiological principles and how they relate to sculling events and training.

ENERGY SYSTEMS

By utilizing the food we eat as a fuel, the body produces energy to function. Food is stored in the body as glycogen and fat. Through chemical reactions, glycogen and fat are used to re-synthesize adenosine triphosphate (ATP). ATP is an energy-carrying molecule that is present in all living cells. ATP is stored in the muscle cell and converted into energy when the muscle is required to perform a contraction. Protein is also used to fuel bodily function but to a much lesser extent than glycogen and fat. If protein usage significantly increases, this is a sign that the body is under excessive stress.

When the physical exertion of the body is at a moderate level, the stored fuels (glycogen and fat) are broken down with oxygen and used to re-synthesize ATP, providing us with energy. At this level, the heart and lungs can supply enough oxygen to support the aerobic metabolism of fats and glycogen or glucose. This process utilizes oxygen and is, therefore, described as 'aerobic'. The waste products are carbon dioxide and water.

When exertion is at an intensive level, or when the energy demand changes rapidly, oxygen supply alone cannot keep up with the breakdown of the stored fuels to supply the body with energy. When this occurs, the body produces energy in an 'anaerobic' (without oxygen) manner. A by-product of this process is a chemical called lactate. This is produced during exercise and is constantly recycled in the body by other active muscle cells with spare aerobic capacity, or in the liver where it is recycled to form glycogen or glucose. It is only when the rate of clearance of lactate from the blood can no longer match its rate of production in the muscle that lactate accumulation will occur. When lactate accumulates in the muscle cell, it will ultimately result in a metabolic acidosis that may be associated with pain and fatigue.

The body requires oxygen to break down this excess lactate into carbon dioxide and water. Therefore, while lactate is accumulating in the blood during exercise, the body is in 'oxygen debt'. Heavy breathing after the exercise has finished, is the body repaying this debt to itself.

Alactic, which means without lactic acid accumulation, is the body's third energy system. It relies on creatine phosphate stored in the muscle cells and is used for activities of extremely short duration, usually up to approximately twenty seconds.

All three of these energy systems are continually active during a 2,000m race, but they have different rates of engagement and different capacities to supply energy to meet the metabolic demand. The alactic system is rapidly engaged but has limited capacity, and is used predominantly in the first 20secs of the race. The aerobic system has the capacity to meet most of the energy demand during the main body of the race but takes between one and two minutes to become fully engaged. During this time the anaerobic system predominates. Although the aerobic system continues to deliver most of the energy during the final sprint, it becomes maximally stressed at this stage, which ultimately leads to fatigue and exhaustion. Therefore, sculling and rowing events are primarily aerobic activities. Due to the aerobic nature of the sport, scullers predominately undertake endurance training.

The body primarily uses its respiratory, circulatory and muscular systems mainly to undertake an aerobic activity. These can be made more effective and efficient through a variety of training methods. The respiratory system draws oxygen from the air through the nose and mouth and into the lungs. In the lungs the oxygen is diffused into the blood through the alveoli. This diffusion moves the oxygen to the blood and into the circulatory system, where the oxygen binds with red blood cells that flow from the larger arteries and branches out through the body down to the smallest of the arteries, which are called capillaries. These capillaries surround the muscle fibre and provide the surface for chemical exchange between the blood and the muscle cell. At this point, the oxygen is diffused across from the haemoglobin in the red blood cell to the mitochondria in the muscle cell, where it is used in the conversion of fuel to energy. There is some research currently looking into the benefit of training the respiratory muscles, although it is commonly believed that the respiratory system is not the limiting factor to an athlete's performance.

Training can improve the circulatory system through the capacity of the heart to sustain high rates of blood flow to the active tissues (cardiac output) and the volume of red blood cells available to deliver oxygen to the muscle fibre, as well as the muscle's efficiency in the uptake of the oxygen. Oxygen utilization training will help when moving into the predominately aerobic body of the race. Steady-state endurance training increases the efficiency of the capillarization process that delivers oxygen to the muscle fibre, as well as removing waste products, such as lactic acid. Oxygen utilization training is generally undertaken with the athlete's heart rate at approximately 75 per cent of maximum. This intensity is kept at this level between 60 and 100min.

The physiological term VO_{2max} describes the measurement of the maximum rate at which the body can take up and use oxygen from the atmosphere. There is a strong correlation between VO_{2max} and 2,000m sculling, rowing and ergo performance. The higher the VO_2, the better the performance. By providing greater capillarization and more oxygen to the muscle cell, oxygen utilization training can also increase the VO_{2max}. Oxygen utilization training is also believed to increase total blood volume.

Interval training between 3 and 8min improves the capacity of the cardiovascular and respiratory systems, which also increases the VO_{2max}. This type of training will promote efficient use of the aerobic capacity during intense effort.

Muscle mass also plays a role in the ability of an athlete to produce a high VO_{2max}. The higher the muscle mass, the higher the VO_2.

This needs to be considered when prescribing a weight-training programme, as weight training can be used to increase muscle mass.

PHYSIOLOGICAL COMPONENTS OF SCULLING EVENTS

Now that you have a basic knowledge of the human body's energy systems, we can explore a little deeper how they relate to the primary events in which scullers participate.

The 2,000m race is predominately aerobic (approximately 80–85 per cent). The race will take between 5min 40s and 8min depending on the boat class. In sculling, as with rowing, the participants face the opposite way to that in which the boat is moving. To gain an advantage, to be able to see the opposition and respond tactically to the opposition, the sculler must sprint from the start. This is predominantly an anaerobic phase, which accumulates lactic acid and places the body in a state of oxygen debt. The lactate and oxygen debt that is accumulated at the start will only subside when the race is over.

There are approximately 230 strokes in a 2,000m sculling race, with each stroke requiring approximately 40kg of force to be applied. This requires a lot of muscle mass, as well as a strong aerobic system, to produce and maintain power in the body of the race.

The final component of the race is the sprint to the finish line. This is where scullers either attempt to defend a lead they have gained or attack a deficit that needs to be reduced. Since

University of London Boat Club, and Leander Club, power away from the starting installation at the 2004 Henley Royal Regatta.

ABOVE: The final of the double-sculls race at the 2004 Henley Royal Regatta, moving through the middle stages of the race under the watchful eye of umpire, Mike Williams.

BELOW: A close finish: the sprint to the line in the men's quadruple-sculls race at the 2004 Henley Royal Regatta.

the aerobic system is already at maximal capacity at this stage of the race, the final sprint is when the anaerobic system becomes maximally stressed. Oxygen debt is at its greatest level and so is lactate accumulation. Lactate tolerance training can assist in the preparation for the demands of the final sprint.

Masters races are primarily over 1,000m. This means that the racing will take approximately 3–4min. Therefore, the anaerobic

ABOVE: The Leander Club's men's quadruple-scull after Hammersmith Bridge during the 2003 Fours Head.

BELOW: Enjoying a pleasant sculling outing.

system will make a larger contribution, coming closer to an equal share of the energy demand. In these shorter races, cardiac output (the amount of blood pumped from the heart) and VO_{2max} are still very important in enabling the sculler to produce enough power consistently over the 1,000m; however, the role of oxygen utilization is reduced in significance.

Long head races that last 20–30min are predominately aerobic and scullers significantly utilize oxygen and work at a high percentage of their VO_{2max} for a longer period of time, than in a 2,000m race. Due to the length of the event, the anaerobic system's role is greatly reduced.

Recreational touring and sculling should be an aerobic activity. Recreational sculling uses the oxygen utilization system, allowing scullers to talk and admire the view of the riverbanks and lake edges.

CHAPTER 7
Training to Improve Your Sculling

Before starting to write your training programme, there are some definitions and training principles that should be understood. Chapter 6 discussed the effects that different types of training have on the body. There is a generally accepted categorization of training zones in rowing.

TRAINING CATEGORIES

There are seven major categories or zones, ranging from short anaerobic sprints to the long-distance oxygen utilization 3 classification. The table (*below*) shows how the various training zones relate to physiological parameters, boat

		Training zones			
Zone	*Stroke rate/min*	*Gold standard time (%)*	*Maximum heart rate (%)*	*Approximate lactate (mmol)*	*Physiological zone definition*
Utilization 3 (U3)	<18	<70	65–75	<1	Below the onset of blood-lactate accumulation
Utilization 2 (U2)	17–18	70–76	65–75	<2	Below the onset of blood-lactate accumulation
Utilization 1 (U1)	19–23	77–82	70–80	2–4	Above the onset of blood-lactate accumulation but below the onset of metabolic acidosis
Anaerobic threshold (AT)	24–28	85–88	82–86	~4	Just below the onset of metabolic acidosis
Transport (TPT)	28–36	88–100	87–95	4–8	Above the onset of metabolic acidosis
Anaerobic (AN)	36+	100+	Maximum		Maximum effort

speed and stroke rate. The aim in training should be to combine fitness and technique in order to match the boat's optimal speed and rate with physiological effort.

TRAINING SPEEDS

The maximum prognostic or gold standard time is a useful tool to guide, monitor and assess an athlete's training and progression. It is also a useful tool to compare different boat categories. A gold standard time is the predicted winning time for an event. It may be 6:32 (5.102m/s) for a men's single-sculler to win a world championship or 7:00 (4.762m/s) for his clubmate to win the men's single-sculls at a national championship.

There is a useful equation that is used to set the training speeds for both club and world championship scullers. By training to a percent-

age of the sculler's gold standard time his progress in training can easily be monitored and assessed. To set the speeds for 500m, which is a manageable and effective distance to monitor in training, the following equation is applied.

$$\frac{Distance~(m) \times 100}{\dfrac{Gold~Standard~Speed~(m/sec)}{\%}} = time~(secs)$$

For example, club sculler's speed at 70%:

$$\frac{500m \times 100}{\dfrac{4.762m/sec}{70\%}} = 2{:}29.99$$

World Championship sculler's speed at 70%:

$$\frac{500m \times 100}{\dfrac{5.102m/sec}{70\%}} = 2{:}20.00$$

Speeds of Club and World Championship scullers related to their training zones

Zone	Stroke rate/min	Gold standard time (%)	Training speed of Club sculler/500m	Training speed of World Championship sculler/500m	Maximum heart rate (%)	Approx. lactate (mmol)
Utilization 3 (U3)	<18	<70	>2:29.99	>2:20.0	60–70	<1
Utilization 2 (U2)	17–18	70–76	2:29.99–2:18.15	2:20.0–2:08.95	65–75	<2
Utilization 1 (U1)	19–23	77–82	2:16.36–2:08.0	2:07.27–1:59.52	75–80	2–4
Anaerobic threshold (AT)	24–28	82–86	2:08.0–2:02.1	1:59.52–1:53.95	80–85	~4
Transport (TPT)	28–36	87–95	2:00.68–1:50.53	1:52.64–1:43.16	85–100	4–8
Anaerobic (AN)	36+	100+	1:45.00+	1:38.00+	Maximum	

The principle of using gold standard times can be applied to junior, school, Masters and club crews. To set the gold standard time, find out what the fastest time is for your targeted event and then think about how fast the race could be rowed in the best possible conditions and predict the winning time.

By including rate into your training zones, you are including the principle of power or distance per stroke that was discussed in Chapter 3. As the boat speed increases through the training zones, it is important to maintain length and rhythm in order to achieve an effective stroke.

If the boat speed is increased through rate rather than power, rhythm will be lost. Conversely, some scullers put all their effort into rowing at the lower zones. This gives a false impression of speed. Training like this usually means the speeds are very fast at low rates but, once moving to a higher intensity, the boat speed cannot be increased with the higher rate.

Smart scullers balance their training intensity between speed, rate and physiological effort.

MONITORING TRAINING INTENSITY

The training zones also relate to the energy systems that were described in Chapter 6. The use of heart-rate monitors and blood-lactate monitoring devices have become common practice in monitoring training. There are some simple ways to do this. More sophisticated scullers use a portable lactate analyser and heart-rate watch to monitor their training. Alternatively, a crude but reasonably accurate way to estimate your maximum heart rate is to subtract your age from 220. You can then calculate at what percentage of your maximum heart rate you should be training.

Watches that display and record heart rates, range from the reasonably straightforward to ones that can download to your computer and review your training session. Alternatively, you can use the method employed by generations of scullers, which involves putting your fingers on to the side of your neck, over your carotid artery, and counting your pulse!

Physiological effects of training at the various training zones						
Effect	*Classification of training zones*					
	U3	U2	U1	AT	TR	AN
Increased blood volume	★★★★	★★★★	★★★	★★	★	
Increased activity of aerobic enzymes	★★★★	★★★★	★★★★	★★★	★★	★
Increased use of fatty acids as a fuel source	★★★★	★★★	★★	★		
Improved ability to use lactate as a fuel	★★	★★	★★★	★★★★	★★★★	★★
Increased maximum rate of muscle glycogen use		★	★★	★★★	★★★★	★★★★
Increased muscle capillarization	★★★★	★★★★	★★★	★★★	★★★	★★
Improved muscle and blood buffering capacity		★	★★	★★★	★★★★	★★★★
Increased maximum cardiac output	★★	★★	★★★	★★★	★★★★	★★★
Increased maximum ventilatory capacity	★	★★	★★	★★★	★★★★	★★★★
Development of race-specific neuromuscular adaptations	★	★	★★	★★	★★★	★★★★

(Adapted from Alan Hahn)

It is important to understand how the different energy systems work and to be clear what you are trying to get out of each training session. Junior and club scullers, who have a limited amount of training time, should consider mixing their training types in the one session. Scullers who have more time for training tend to have one physiological focus for each session.

The majority of training should be aerobic. The reason is two-fold: apart from the enormous physiological benefits already stated, aerobic intensity is where the greatest technical changes can be made.

PERIODIZATION

The training year is divided into the following four stages or phases: preparation, pre-competition, competition and transition. October to March is generally considered to be the preparation phase; April and May, pre-competition; and June to August the competition phase. This is followed by an important post-season regeneration phase (transition).

Due to the aerobic nature of sculling competition, it is important to maintain aerobic training throughout the whole year. This will maintain your endurance base during the pre-competition and competition phases. As can be seen in the table (*see* p.76), the training intensity builds as the training moves to being more specific to racing in the competition phase.

The principle of periodization is to allow for the training programme to ebb and flow, providing the athlete with the structure to adapt to the training stimulus. Simply put, the body is placed under physiological stress when training takes place. When resting after training, the body recovers and adapts to the training stimulus. If there is sufficient recovery, the body prepares itself through physiological adaptations to better handle the training stimuli. By periodizing the training, you will adapt to a load: through the next training cycle the stimulus is increased and a further adaptation occurs. With good training programmes, scullers and rowers continue to improve their physiology even after ten years of training. As a result of these adaptations, it is possible to

---

Examples of workloads and training sessions in the seven training zones (*see* Appendix I for sample training sessions)

Zone	Type of training	Sample session
U3	Long, low-level aerobic training in excess of 120min	120min cross-training/cycling 120min sculling rate 16
U2	60–120min steady state aerobic exercise	60–120min sculling rate 18
U1	20–40min continuous rowing	2 × 20min rating 19/21/23/19 every 2min with 10min off in-between sets
AT	8–20min	1 × 5km rating 24
TPT	2–8min pieces in interval fashion	3 × 2,000m rate 26/28 28/30 32 Rest = 10min
AN	Sprint training	2 × (6 × 1min on 1min off R34–38) Rest between sets = 10min

Recommended training zone percentages for each phase				
	Preparation (%) (October–March)	Pre-competition (%) (April–May)	Competition (%) (June–July)	Transition (%) (September)
U3	10			
U2	67	57.5	66	100
U1	12	29	20	
AT	6	6	4	
TPT	4	6	8	
AN	1	1.5	2	

train longer, harder and produce more power. However, if the training stimulus is maintained for too long or too intensely, the athlete may break down. Having the correct balance between work (or training), rest and recovery will allow training adaptation to take place.

Preparation Phase

During the preparation phase, the training aims are to maximize the sculler's endurance base, consolidate strength gains in the gym and lay a strong technical foundation. The percentage of training time in the utilization zones reflects the importance endurance plays on sculling performance. During this phase, you should improve your mental skills. Visualization techniques can help to make technical improvements and sound goal-setting strategies will enable you to maximize your training and to build your confidence. Specific mental-skills strategies are covered in depth in Chapter Eight.

Pre-Competition Phase

The aim of the pre-competition phase is to apply the power, rhythm and endurance developed through the preparation phase to the racing performance. This phase will include early season regattas. Due to the nature of the training phase, which is to prepare for racing, the training gains are made in the boat and are race-specific. There should be less gym, cross-training and ergometer sessions, and more time spent on the water. Again, the training has a significant aerobic utilization component but, significantly, more at the higher level and more training at close to race intensity. Weight training should be maintained and good technique must be emphasized as the training intensity increases. You should develop your race strategies throughout this phase. Visualization can also be used to assist in race-strategy development. A mental-skills programme should develop a robust review, plan and implement cycle to lay the foundation for your thinking during the racing season.

Competition Phase

This phase generally lasts between two and four weeks. Its aim is to make the training race-specific and to optimize performance. This is the phase with the greatest percentage of anaerobic and transport training. Aerobic training is still required to maintain endurance, to assist with recovery from the increased intensity and to provide enough utilization training to maintain technical improvement. Goal-setting skills are refined during this period and you should begin taking ownership and responsibility for your performance.

The competition phase also includes the tapering period into the major regattas. A taper is a period of approximately two weeks prior to a major regatta. The aim of the taper is to reduce any residual fatigue from training, whilst increasing confidence, and fine-tuning boat speed and race strategy. Timed correctly throughout the regatta, the optimal performance will be produced in the final. Training volume should be reduced to approximately half. Racing pieces should focus on quality rather than quantity and be thoroughly reviewed, so that you can practise your race strategy. Consistency in the taper produces consistency in the racing (*see* Appendix II for a sample two-week taper).

Transition Phase

The aim of the transition period between one season and the next is to allow the time to regenerate both physically and mentally. You should undertake light aerobic activity, minimize your time in the boat and take a break from the pressures of racing.

REVERSIBILITY

There is also the training principle of reversibility. This states that if the training stimulus decreases, then the body finds its homeostasis (natural resting level) at a lower level. This results in a decreased training and work level. Therefore, the training programme must have a built-in training stimulus. Training cycles occur at three main levels: meso, macro and micro. In practical terms, this means: annually, monthly and weekly.

Meso Cycle

The four-year Olympic cycle is a meso cycle. It will have specific objectives throughout the four years. There is usually a turnover of athletes in Olympic programmes after each Olympic regatta. The four-year cycle will reflect new athletes coming into the programme and the base preparation that is required for success at the highest level. The table (*below*) demonstrates this cycle, as the training objectives move from the general to the specific during the four years.

Macro Cycle

A macro cycle generally lasts between four and six weeks. It has a weekly building phase that is followed by an unloading period. The preparation phase of the macro cycle lasts longer than in the competition phase. This is done to provide an optimal training stimulus during the former and an optimal recovery during the latter phase. Volume should be increased by no more than 5 per cent each week. The unloading

A meso cycle	
Year	*Training objective*
1	Base endurance
	General strength
	General racing concepts
2	Base endurance
	General strength
	General racing strategies
3	Specific endurance
	Specific strength
	General racing strategies
4	Specific endurance
	Specific strength
	Specific-race strategy

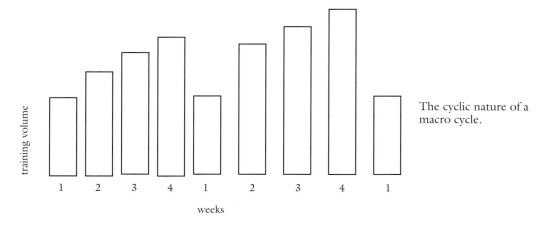

The cyclic nature of a macro cycle.

Micro cycles for athletes at three different levels							
	Mon	*Tues*	*Wed*	*Thurs*	*Fri*	*Sat*	*Sun*
School athletes	1	1	1	1	1	2	0
Club/Master's athletes	0	2	1	2	1	2	2
Full-time athletes	3	2	1	3	2	2	0

phase should be approximately 50 per cent of volume of the phase's maximum week. When planning the unloading period, the coach or sculler needs to acknowledge that fatigue is the accumulation of training in the preceding month. The heavier the training loads, the greater the need for effective recovery during the unloading period. The cyclic nature of the macro cycle is demonstrated in the figure above.

Micro Cycle

A micro cycle reflects the training flow of the week. The volume and cycle is usually determined by the time available for training. As with the macro cycle, the micro cycle has a flow of loading and unloading components. Micro cycles for athletes at three different levels are demonstrated in the table (*above*). The

figures relate to the number of training sessions. A good practice during the micro cycle is to follow intensive training sessions with aerobic training. This will assist in the athlete's recovery and training adaptation.

VOLUME

The training volume is generally determined by the amount of time available for training. Scullers need to possess good time-management skills. It is always a difficult task to balance training, study, work, family and a social life. Regardless of the volume, the training zone ratios should be observed. If a Master's athlete can only train four or five times a week, then the training should reflect the energy contribution of the event. Half of the

Training volumes	
Level	*Hours/week*
International	18–30
Senior club	14–18
Top juniors and intermediate club	12–16
Schools and junior club	5–12

training should be aerobic and half should be at an anaerobic threshold or higher. Being primarily an endurance sport, it takes a lot of training time to gain the physiological and technical attributes to become successful in sculling and rowing.

These hours refer to actual training time, not travel to and from training. When setting training volumes, the coach and sculler have to consider for how many years the sculler has been training, as well as aspirations and availability. It is important, especially for adolescents, to build gradually and not to be too ambitious. Young people need to enjoy what they do in order to maintain their interest and enjoyment in the sport. Excessive training can also make them more susceptible to injury and have a detrimental effect on their schoolwork. The Amateur Rowing Association has established sound recommendations for the training of young people (*table overleaf*).

It is important that you should progress through training at your own level and that the training programme should be tailored to suit your individual needs. Of course, in crew boats there will always have to be some flexibility in setting a training programme, in order to balance the needs of all the members. However, individual sessions in a single scull and on land can help to address imbalances or specific weaknesses. The single sculler can have a totally individualized programme to suit his needs.

WRITING A TRAINING PROGRAMME

When writing a training programme, you must first ascertain what it is that you are trying to achieve. This may be success at a single event, such as a head race, Henley Royal Regatta, national schools championships, World Championships or even the Olympic Games. Alternatively, it could be a series of events, pennant points or a world cup series.

Constructing, developing, selling and implementing a training programme is a cyclic process, each phase of which will involve elements of planning, implementation, monitoring and reviewing. It is important that the season's goal is realistic and achievable, and that the requirements of the level of training necessary to achieve success are clearly understood. These factors will determine how elaborate the training programme will be. Your training history, race results, skills, physiological capacity, mental skills and availability to train and compete, will all determine the level at which you will compete. These goals should be long (annual), medium (monthly) and short (weekly) term.

Planning

Once the main goal of the season has been established, and the strengths and weaknesses of the scullers assessed, planning can commence. Using a diary, either electronic or old-fashioned paper, start at the competition you are aiming for and work back.

- First, enter in any dates that will affect the training programme, such as regattas, national squad or regional requirements, and school holidays.
- Identify the aims of the regattas throughout the season. Which ones are you going to target and taper for? Which ones you will train through and not taper for.

ARA training recommendations

Age group/age	Number of coached sessions/week	Content and breakdown of the sessions	Comments
J11/11	1 maximum	Skills and technique	Short sessions based on time on the water, rather than distance covered.
J12/12	2 maximum	Skills and technique	Short sessions based on time on the water, rather than distance covered.
J13/13	3 maximum	2 on water 1 on land Skills and technique	Remember that sculling may not be the young athletes' only leisure-time activity.
J14/14	4 maximum	2–3 on water 1–2 on land Skills and technique	
J15/15	4–6	4 on water 1–2 on land	Athletes are starting to learn to train properly. Please ensure qualified people teach weight-lifting technique, if this is included in the programme. Keep the sessions short as the athletes get tired and cannot concentrate for long periods.
J16/16	6–8	4–5 on water 2 strength training 1–2 cross-training	Remember that with GCSEs approaching, this is a big year academically for the athletes who are still learning how to train properly.
J17/17–J18/18	7–8 10–14 if training for a national team*	7–8 on water 2–3 strength training 2–3 cross-training	Should be developing good base endurance and strength. One training-free day a week is recommended. Some sessions can be short, such as a 30-min ergo test.

*The number of sessions assumes that the athlete is in a training-camp environment with no other distractions.

- Divide the season into preparation and competition phases. Calculate what percentages of the training zones you want to spend in each phase.

- Starting with the most important regatta and working back, calculate how many hours training you will do in each of the weeks in each phase. This should follow the principles of periodization.

- Establish the phases in which strength and resistance training will take priority and the ones where a maintenance programme will suffice.
- Schedule in the testing dates. Testing is required to monitor the progress through each of the training phases. This monitoring should be done on the water, on the ergometer and in the gym.

Once you have the plan laid out, sell the concepts of the programme to the athletes. To gain the maximum benefit from the training programme, the sculler must exploit what the programme offers, rather than be a passive recipient. Regularly evaluate and modify the programme and individualize it as much as possible to suit each sculler's needs. Importantly, keep a detailed diary, so that you can accurately reflect on what you have actually done rather than what you think you have done.

Resistance Training

This can take many forms and is a very effective way to supplement training on the water. It can improve performance and assist in injury prevention. It can improve general physical development, particularly strength and power; improve sculling technique; and correct muscle imbalances.

There are many myths and fads involved with resistance training. Some rowing and sculling coaches, and their training programmes, do not advocate any training with weights. The thinking behind this is that extra muscle mass and strength can reduce the technical ability, that strength is a minor contributor in a predominately endurance sport, or simply that weights are unsafe. Rowing is both a power and endurance sport, and it is advisable to train both these components.

Weight training, done correctly, will improve your sculling. Technique is as important in the gym as it is on the water. Resistance and weight training are quite safe as long as progression is gradual and good technique is taught, this includes being safe for youngsters.

When considering whether exercises should be done with free weights or machines, the coach and sculler should consider the benefits of both methods. Free weights offer a balance component that can strengthen ligaments and joints, as well as promoting body awareness. Machines provide a safer environment for heavy maximal strength efforts and the ability to load one side more than the other in order to address strength imbalances, for example a one-legged leg press.

Weight training for strength gain can be very helpful, especially with the explosive start of the race. For the 1,000m Masters sculler, this holds even more importance than the longer 2,000m and head races. Strength gains and general athletic development also make the sculler more robust and better able to cope with the rigours of the on-water training.

Because most rowing events are over 2,000m, and given the speed of the drive phase of the rowing stroke is between $\frac{5}{10}$ and $\frac{6}{10}$th of a second, power training is very important. Power is the rate of doing work. It is of little value to train the body to move as slowly as when heavily laden with a weights bar that causes you to lift in slow motion. The drive phase of the sculling stroke is a lot quicker and more dynamic. There are exercises that can be done in the gym to enhance the specific muscles that are used in sculling and rowing. The power clean, squat and bench pull are all excellent exercises that will develop the body to apply more power to the stroke.

There are also non-specific exercises that strengthen the antagonist and supporting muscles. Working these groups of muscles helps to develop stronger structures for the muscles that are activated to apply power during the stroke.

The drive phase of the rowing stroke requires extension of the knees and hips, while the recovery phase involves the flexion of the same joints. In general, scullers and rowers are a lot stronger in extension than they are in flexion. This lopsided extension/flexion ratio may be a reason for the onset of lower back pain amongst rowers. Resistance training of the abdominal and gluteal muscles can help rectify this imbalance.

It is always important to be clear about what you want to achieve through resistance training. It may be hypertrophy (the increase of the lean muscle mass), power, strength, lactate tolerance, or balanced general development and endurance.

When programming resistance training, the best starting point is the off-season. Progress your resistance training through hypertrophy, power and general strength to maximal strength and then to circuits. Endurance weights can be done as a cross-training session throughout the preparation phase. When undertaking a weights programme, the adaptations made will be neural as well as muscular. Gains will not be retained if the strength training is stopped for long periods of time. These are mainly believed to be neural changes. Therefore, weight training should be done from the preparation to competition phase of training, and should be a core component of the training programme.

As the rowing season gets closer, the exercises in the programme should move from the general to the more rowing-specific. Scullers have a scull in each hand and the power from the legs and trunk comes evenly through both shoulders and arms. Consequently, they need stronger upper bodies than sweep rowers. This should be reflected in the resistance programme, with particular attention being paid to the development of the shoulders and arms.

	Strength	Power	Hypertrophy	Circuit training	Endurance
Set and repetition requirements					
Sets	3–4	4–6	4–6	3–6	1–6
Repetitions	2–6	6–10	10–15	20–30	30–50
Intensity from max (%)	90–100	60–70	75–85	40–50	30–40
Speed of lift	Slow	Dynamic	Dynamic to slow through set	Dynamic	Dynamic
Sessions per week	2–4	2–3	2–3	2–3	2–3

Hypertrophy

The building of lean mass is often a difficult task. In scullers with a limited training background, hypertrophy can occur with regular and general training. For older or more experienced athletes, it is harder to achieve. To gain lean muscle mass it is necessary to undertake a weights programme that targets the big muscle groups and increases the size of the largest number of muscles. By targeting the quadriceps, gluteal and latissimus dorsi muscles you will be able to make an increase in size to the largest number of muscle fibres.

To make a hypertrophic change, you have to reduce the amount of endurance training and undertake at least four weights sessions a week. The weights programme can be divided into upper body and lower body sessions. To maximize the muscles' recovery, the weight sessions should be alternated between upper body and lower body during the week. Each set should contain between ten and fifteen repetitions, the last few of which should be a struggle to achieve. Rest periods between sets must be shortened to approximately 30s in order to elicit fatigue. This places the muscles under the greatest load, and regeneration and muscle building will follow. If time for full recovery between sets is allowed, there will not be enough stimulus for the muscle to grow. Endurance training while the muscles are regenerating will hamper hypertrophy.

To maximize the effects of the weights, the volume of training on the water has to be significantly reduced. There is a real conundrum when balancing the need for hypertrophic gain and the need for an improvement in an individual's endurance capacity. It is extremely difficult to achieve both.

Nutrition also has a major role to play. When aiming to increase lean muscle mass, the number and type of calories consumed must be increased. Protein is particularly important, as it assists with the building of muscle in the body. Some form of protein and carbohydrate should be eaten as soon as possible after each training session. This not only refuels the muscles with glycogen but also assists in the repair and building, which promotes hypertrophy.

Power

Power is defined as the rate of doing work and power training is the most effective method of weight training to improve sculling performance. As with sculling, power weights have a dynamic speed component to them. Power weights have sets of between six and ten repetitions; each one has to be dynamic. To keep the movement dynamic, the weights are not as heavy as they would be for strength weights. By not being a maximal effort, the power weights are closer to sculling training and racing on the water, where each stroke is close to, but not at, maximal effort.

Power weights best reflect and compliment what is trying to be achieved in training on the water. These weight-training sessions should also include exercises that complement the sculling action. Technically, power cleans are a very similar action to the rowing and sculling stroke; for this reason power cleans are a valuable exercise to do in the gym. It is important that the power clean is taught well. Your power-clean technique will show similar technical problems to those that you display on the water. Squats, both with the weight resting on the back, as well as the bar resting on the front over the collarbone, mirror the driving hip extension action of sculling. Isolating the sculling arm draw with the bench-pull exercise also targets the arm draw required in sculling and rowing.

The aim of power training is very similar to achieving a powerful stroke and is an effective use of gym training.

Sample upper-body hypertrophy programme

Exercise	Repetitions/set	Repetitions/set	Repetitions/set	Repetitions/set
Lateral pull	15	15	15	15
Bench press	15	15	12	12
Chin-up with weights	15	15	15	15
Bench pull	15	15	12	12
Dip with weights	15	15	15	15
Seated rowing	15	15	12	12
Abdominal work	40	40	40	40

Sample lower-body hypertrophy programme

Exercise	Repetitions/set	Repetitions/set	Repetitions/set	Repetitions/set
Power clean	15	15	12	12
Back squat	15	15	12	12
Leg extension	15	15	15	15
Dead lift	15	15	12	12
Hamstring curl	15	15	15	15
Front squat	15	15	12	12
Abdominal work	40	40	40	40

Power-weights programme

Exercise	Repetitions/ set	Repetitions/ set	Repetitions/ set	Repetitions/ set	Repetitions/ set
Power clean	10	10	8	8	6
Bench press	8	8	6	6	6
Squat	10	10	8	8	6
Bench pull	10	10	8	8	6
Lateral pull	10	10	8	8	6
Three-way back exercise	10	10	10	10	10
Dead lift	10	10	8	8	6
Chin-up	10	10	10	10	10
Back extension	10	10	10	10	10
Abdominal work	40	40	40	40	40

Power Training on the Water

Power training can also be done on the water. Resistance may be added to the boat by either tying a cord or band around the hull, or purchasing a sea anchor. The increased drag will add resistance to the run of the boat. Rowing as hard as possible, you should be able to complete between ten to twenty strokes at a low rating (between 12 and 14 strokes/min). Row light in-between the work sets with the same number of strokes rowed with full pressure. A well-trained sculler should be able to manage up to 400 power strokes in one training session. Racing-starts with added resistance to the boat is also effective power training. The advantage power strokes have over other forms of resistance training is that they are sculling-specific.

Strength

This can be a very risky method of weight training. As the weights being lifted are extremely heavy, technique is put under a lot of pressure. In fact, it may be technique rather than strength that is the limiting factor in lifting the weight. When very heavy weights are being lifted, the risk of injury is increased. It is, therefore, important that it is done with a partner and that good technique is observed. There is great debate about the relevance of maximal strength benefiting the performance of an event that lasts 2,000m. There is no doubt that maximal strength will help the explosive start in the first 20sec, which is particularly advantageous to Masters who race over 1,000m. However, it is the power applied over the duration of the race that will maximize performance. The power equation is force multiplied by acceleration, and force is strength divided by time. As strength is a major component of power, strength training should be a component of training. A strength increase will increase the force component of the power equation, therefore increasing the power capacity.

Strength training is done with repetitions of between two and six lifts with plenty of rest time in-between. There should be approximately six exercises in the session so that you do not become overly fatigued and unable to apply a maximal effort. Exercises for strength training include the power clean, squats, dead lift, bench pull and bench press.

Sample strength-weights programme			
Exercise	Repetitions/set	Repetitions/set	Repetitions/set	Repetitions/set
Power clean	5	5	4	4
Bench press	6	6	5	5
Back squat	5	5	4	4
Bench pull	6	6	5	5
Dead lifts	5	5	4	4
Chin-up with weights	6	6	4	4
Leg press	5	5	4	4
Abdominal work	40	40	40	40

Circuit Training

There are approximately 230 strokes in a 2,000m sculling race. Each stroke will require the application of approximately 40kg of force. To achieve this, a well-developed muscle mass and a strong cardiovascular system are needed to produce and maintain power. A weights circuit can assist in developing the ability to cope with the intensity of a 2,000m race. This type of circuit work trains the body to build and tolerate lactate acid. If you are able to monitor this type of training with lactate analysers and heart-rate monitors, you will find that, generally, you can produce very high lactates. Each round of the circuit should last between 6 and 7min. The rest between each circuit should be long enough for the heart rate to drop below 120 beats/min. The most technically challenging exercises should be scheduled early in the circuit; otherwise there is a risk that technique may be compromised by fatigue.

Endurance Weights

Cross-training has increased in popularity as a training tool. Cross-country skiing, cycling, running, swimming and the use of cardio sections of the gym, have all been used to supplement the aerobic training a sculler or rower has to do. The change of training and environment is often a welcome break. Weight training with lighter weights and body-weight exercises provides a good tool for an aerobic session. These circuits can provide a wide variety of exercises to keep the athletes motivated, while also providing a well-balanced weights programme. The exercises that are chosen will often depend on what is available at the gym. Once around the circuit should take between 20 and 30min. As each exercise takes a different amount of time, between 75 and 90s should be spent at each station. The circuit should have between three and five sets. Technique should again be emphasized for the duration of the circuit.

EXERCISES: WEIGHT TRAINING

POWER CLEAN

Stand over the bar with your feet underneath at hip width. The bar should almost be touching your shins. Look forward and up with your back set, shoulders down and lower abdominal muscles drawn down. Bend your knees and

Sample circuit			
Exercise	*Men (kg)*	*Women (kg)*	*Repetitions*
Power clean	45	35	30
Bench press	45	30	30
Back squat	60	50	30
Bench pull	45	30	30
Squat jump			30
Lateral pull-down	45	30	30
Sit-up	10	5	30
Back extension	20	10	30

Sample endurance-weights circuit

Exercise	Recommended: men	Recommended: women
Power clean	30kg	20kg
Full squat	40kg	30kg
Ergo	Power strokes rate 16	Power strokes rate 16
Bench press	30kg	20kg
Lateral pull-down	40kg	30kg
Leg press	50kg	40kg
Single-arm row	15kg	7.5kg
Squat jump	10kg	5kg
Dumb-bell clean	10kg	5kg
Dumb-bell bench press	15kg	10kg
Full squat	40kg	30kg
Ergo	Power strokes rate 16	Power strokes rate 16
Step-up	10kg	5kg
45-degree sit and twist medicine ball sit-up	Medicine ball	Medicine ball
High pull on block	20kg	10kg

POWER CLEAN

ABOVE: Set your back and have the bar close to your shins.

RIGHT: Accelerate your gluteal muscles and drive through your hips to accelerate the bar off the floor.

FAR RIGHT: Shrug your shoulders to keep the bar accelerating, swing your elbows away from you catching the bar on your deltoids and clavicle.

Power Clean

This exercise develops most of the major muscles and muscle groups including the:

- quadriceps;
- gluteal muscle group;
- hamstrings;
- pectoralis;
- latissimus dorsi;
- deltoids;
- biceps;
- triceps;
- trapezius;
- gastrocnemius.

grasp the bar at shoulder width. Take a breath and using your legs, lift the bar off the floor. As the bar passes your knees, drive through your hips, this will accelerate the bar until you are standing at full extension, having risen up on your toes and shrugged your shoulders. Allow the bar to continue rising while you bend your arms and drop under the bar, catching it across the top of the anterior deltoids and clavicle.

Once the bar is resting across your deltoids, you can exhale and take a short breath. To put the weight down, keep your back set with good posture and lower the bar to your knees, then on to the floor.

BACK SQUAT

It is always safer to pick the bar off a squat rack rather than the floor when doing back squats. Step under the squat rack and rest the bar across your back on the trapezius muscles, take a deep

Back Squat

This exercise develops the following muscles and muscle groups:

- quadriceps;
- gluteals;
- hamstrings;
- calf muscles;
- postural muscles of the back and abdomen.

BACK SQUAT Your feet should be shoulder-width apart and toes level. This is the start and finish position of the back squat.

Maintain your back position as you squat down and drive up.

BENCH PULL At the start and finish position of the bench pull your arms should be able to hang straight. You may need to adjust the height of the bench to achieve this.

Use your arms to lift the bar and do not let your chin or legs lift off the bench.

breath and set your back. Step out from the rack looking forward and up. Bend your knees and slowly lower yourself down until your knees are at 90 degrees. Drive through your hips until you are standing at full extension.

BENCH PULL

Lying flat on a bench with the bar underneath you, activate the latissimus dorsi and bicep muscles to lift the bar and hit the bottom of the bench. It is important that your chin and legs stay in contact with the bench. If they lift up during the pull, then you are using your back extensors to lift the weight rather than the correct arm and shoulder muscles. If this occurs, the weight is probably too heavy for you to lift and you should select a lighter weight.

THREE-WAY BACK EXERCISE

The three-way back exercise promotes shoulder stability. Lying with your chest flat on the bench, retract the scapula and with controlled movements and slightly bent arms, swing your arms away from you and back. Then, behind and back, and finally, forward and back. The scapula should stay retracted through all three directions.

Bench Pull

This exercise develops the following muscle groups:

- latissimus dorsi;
- teres major;
- rhomboids;
- biceps.

Three-Way Back Exercise

This exercise develops the following muscle groups:

- teres major;
- teres minor;
- infraspinatous;
- levator scapulae;
- rhomboids;
- deltoids.

Draw your shoulder blades (scapula) down and in to set your shoulders before you start the exercise.

Swing your arms laterally away from you whilst keeping your shoulders in the set position. The set scapula will limit your range of movement.

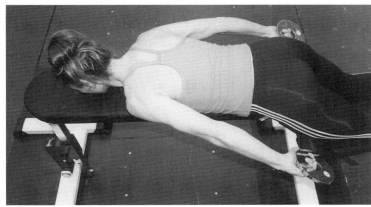

Swing your arms back whilst keeping your scapula set.

Swing your arms forward whilst maintaining your set scapula.

'GOOD MORNINGS'

'Good mornings' are very good for developing correct patterning and development of the flexion and extension action required in sculling. Place the bar across the trapezius muscle, as you

---

'Good Morning'

This exercise develops the following muscle groups:

- gluteal muscles;
- hamstrings;
- erectores spinale.

---

would for a back squat. Breathe in and bend forward from the hips by activating the gluteal muscles and drawing in with the lower abdominal muscles. You should bend over until your body is parallel to the floor, then, by using the gluteal and spinal erectors, extend back up until you are standing. You can do 'good mornings' with either bent or straight legs and you should feel the hamstrings stretch.

SINGLE-ARM ROW

Kneeling on a bench with your supporting shoulder fixed and back flat, lift the dumbbell to your chest and lower. Make sure that your shoulder has initiated the lift and that your postural muscles have held your trunk stable.

Stand tall and maintain good body posture.

Activating your gluteal and lower abdominal muscles, bend over. You should feel a stretch in your hamstring muscles.

Single-Arm Row

This exercise develops the following muscle groups:

- rhomboids;
- teres major;
- latissimus dorsi;
- deltoids;
- biceps;
- abdominal and postural muscles.

SEATED ROW (ARMS ONLY)

With your knees bent and body upright and stable, draw the handle towards you by activating the latissimus dorsi and biceps muscles. Row arms with controlled movements and good posture for the required number of repetitions.

Seated Row

This exercise develops the following muscle groups:

- rhomboids;
- deltoids;
- latissimus dorsi;
- erector spinae;
- biceps;
- abdominal postural muscles.

EXERCISES: TRUNK STRENGTHENING

Due to the extension component of the sculling and rowing stroke, imbalances can develop between the abdomen and hips (flexion) and the hips and back (extension). This can not only lead to injury but also compromise you from getting into the most effective drive position.

You need to develop an awareness of the quads and gluteal muscles being activated at the finish of the stroke. Keeping the gluteal muscles activated, pull in the lower abdominal muscles and 'rock over' from the pelvis and lumbar spine, move from the finish position and commence sliding forward. This activation sequence will result in a good pattern of lumbar–pelvic rhythm that will increase trunk length and control from the pelvis and lumbar spine, rather than locking through the pelvis and hinging through the lumbar spine. With a good lumbar–pelvic rhythm, where the ratio of the pelvis and lumbar spine rotates forwards or backwards, you will approach the front turn of the stroke and be able to maintain a strong trunk position and commence the drive phase with the use of the strong gluteal muscles. This produces a more effective drive phase that will not affect your back and enhances the use of some of the most powerful muscles in the body.

Many scullers and rowers do not utilize their gluteal and lower abdominal muscles enough. Instead, they rely on their hamstrings and hip flexors. Again, a high level of body awareness is very important – if your hamstrings and hip flexors feel tight, it is likely that you need to strengthen the gluteal and lower abdominal muscles while stretching the hamstrings and hip flexors.

Due to the muscle synergy involved in the functioning and support of the pelvis and lower back, the most effective way to strengthen around the hip and lower back area is through strengthening the lower abdominal and gluteal muscles through complex exercises. 'Complex' refers to exercises that do not just isolate one particular muscle but work a combination of muscles. Once the lower abdominal and gluteal muscles have been strengthened, the aim should be to increase the endurance capacity of these muscle groups.

The following exercises will strengthen the gluteal and abdominal muscles. They can be

Lie down with your legs at 90 degrees, with your knees and feet over your hips.

done in a circuit format, at home while watching television, or as part of a weights programme. In one form or another, it is recommended that at least some of these exercises are done daily.

REVERSE CURL

Lying on your back with arms by your side and legs at 90 degrees, draw the lower abdominal muscles down and activate the gluteal muscles. With the small of your back flat on the ground, your legs will rise slightly. This exercise will work the lower abdominal and gluteal muscles.

ABDOMINAL CURL TO CATCH POSITION

Sit with knees bent, draw in on the lower abdominal muscles to maintain the lumbar–pelvis rhythm and sit up into the catch position. You should come up to three catch positions. Straight up into the sculling catch position, then to the left (bow side) and right (stroke side). This exercise will develop the lower

Activate your lower abdominal muscles to draw your legs up. Your legs will not move far; avoid your legs swinging.

Keeping your shoulders relaxed, bring yourself up to the sculling catch position by activating your gluteal and lower abdominal muscles.

Bring yourself up to the stroke side (right) catch position.

Bring yourself up to the bow side (left) catch position.

abdominal, rectus abdominus, oblique and gluteal muscles.

THE PLANK

Resting on your elbows and toes, draw in the lower abdominals, while activating the gluteal and back extensor muscles to firm your trunk. Be careful to maintain level hips and a rigid trunk. This exercise will work the lower abdominal, back extensor and gluteal muscles.

HORIZONTAL HOLD

Lie on your side, resting on your elbow and heels while keeping your hips even. Draw in the lower abdominal muscles while maintaining this position. This can be made more difficult by resting on your hand rather than your elbow, or by raising your leg. The exercise will work your shoulders, lower abdominal, oblique and gluteal muscles.

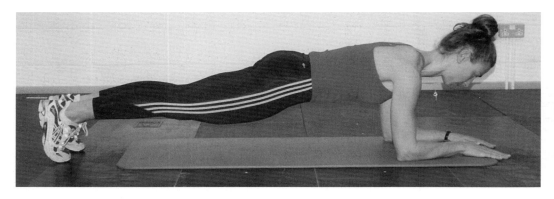

The plank is an isometric strengthening exercise. An isometric exercise is where the muscle is activated but does not lengthen or shorten. It remains static.

ABOVE LEFT: The horizontal hold is another isometric exercise. It will develop your shoulder stability, as well as your abdominal and gluteal muscles.

ABOVE: Add a degree of difficulty by adding leg weights and rest on your hand instead of your elbow.

LEFT: Moving into a star position with leg weights while maintaining good posture will test the strongest sculler.

Push-ups on the gym ball add balance and control to your upper body training.

Lower your chest right down to the ball.

PUSH-UP FROM GYM BALL

Hold your hands on either side of the gym ball, with your arms straight and feet in contact with the ground. Activate your lower abdominals to make your trunk rigid and remember to keep your hips level. Bend your arms and lower yourself on to the ball then push-up by straightening your arms. By doing the push-up on a gym ball you are adding a balance dimension. Be careful to maintain your trunk position. This exercise will develop your chest (pectoralis major) and arm muscles (triceps).

LEG LOWERING

Lying on your side, resting your head on your hand, raise and lower your straight leg. Be careful to keep your hips level by drawing in the lower abdominal muscles. To add a degree of difficulty to this exercise, try adding ankle weights to your legs. Once you can handle the weights, bend your knee and straighten while lowering your leg. This exercise will strengthen the maximus and medis gluteal muscles.

Make sure you rest your head on your palm.

Control your breathing throughout the exercise.

LUNGE

Stand with your feet together. While maintaining your good back position and level hips, lunge forward with your lead leg putting your weight through this leg, leaving the back foot stationary. The knee of the lead leg should finish at 90 degrees. To increase the difficulty of the exercise, hold weights in your hand or step on to a wobble cushion. This

FAR LEFT: Stand evenly on both feet with your toes level before starting to lunge.

LEFT: Make sure your hips stay level when you lunge. Holding your hands on your hips while you lunge can help you feel if your hips are level.

exercise will develop the gluteal and quadriceps muscles.

STEP-UPS

Stand with good posture in front of a box that is the same approximate height as your knee. Step on top of the box then step down, being careful to keep your hips level. To increase the difficulty of this exercise, hold weights in your hands or raise the height of the box. This exercise will develop the gluteal and quadricep muscles.

SQUAT WITH A BALL AGAINST THE WALL

Rest a gym ball between your back and a wall. Keeping your hips level and good back posture, squat down until your knee is at a 45-degree angle. Drive through your hips until you are standing again. To make this exercise more difficult, try holding weights while you squat, squatting with one leg and then attaching ankle weights on your non-squatting leg. This exercise will develop the gluteal, quadriceps and abdominal as well as your postural muscles.

SQUAT ON A WOBBLE CUSHION

Stand on a wobble cushion. Once you have found your balance, squat down until your knees are at 45 degrees and drive through your hips so that you return to the standing position. Be careful to maintain good posture and level hips. This exercise improves your balance as well as developing the gluteal and quadriceps muscles.

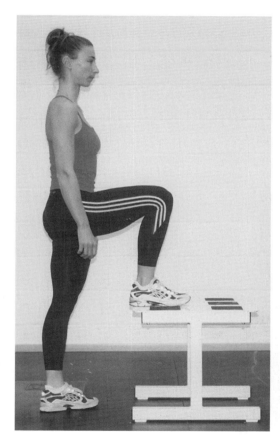

Step up onto a block keeping your hips level all the time.

Using a gym ball, squat against a wall while maintaining level hips and good posture.

While finding your balance, maintain level hips and good posture.

Time the swing up of the arms and your hips rolling forward as you would in the boat.

GYM BALL TO CATCH POSITION

Sit on top of the gym ball on the front of your ischial tuberosity bone in your pelvis. Hold an elastic cord with both hands, while your feet anchor the cord to the floor. Roll up into the catch position; roll back, then back up into the catch position. Be careful to maintain good posture and low shoulders. This exercise will improve your balance and co-ordination and develop the postural muscles.

SUSPENDED ERGOMETER

Using a chain, rope or boat tie, tie the handle of the ergometer to the chain guard. With the handle stationary, set and suspend yourself in the correct catch position. Activate the gluteal muscles to lift yourself off the seat; you should feel the suspension through the latissimus

dorsi muscle. The exercise is isometric (muscles activating but staying the same length), so to increase the level of difficulty, you should increase the suspension time. The illustration (*above*) shows the handle set further through the stroke. Whilst working the same muscle group, it is harder to maintain good suspension and keep your buttocks off the seat in this second position. This exercise will develop body awareness, as well as the gluteal, quadricep and latissimus dorsi muscles.

EXERCISES: FLEXIBILITY AND STRETCHING

Flexibility allows the joints and muscles to move through their full range of movement (ROM) and therefore provide length to the stroke when sculling. Being inflexible through the hips and shoulders not only shortens the range of movement that can be achieved, but can increase the likelihood of injury, as the necessity to scull outside of your natural ROM will place undue stress on other joints. Being too flexible may also lead to injuries. Over-reaching and over-compressing in the catch position can cause excessive loading of the back and knees.

Scullers who have trained to achieve a well-balanced, muscular body that can produce a lot of power and is flexible enough to scull with good length, will be able to maximize their performance through sculling correctly. Age,

ABOVE: You must feel the gluteal muscles lift off the seat.

LEFT: It is a lot harder to achieve suspension in the late-drive position. You will have to feel the quadriceps and gluteal muscles to lift off the seat.

injuries, muscle bulk, disease and joint structure all determine an individual's flexibility. Flexibility can also change from joint to joint or muscle group to muscle group – you might have flexible hamstrings and tight shoulders or vice versa. Evidence that flexibility alone reduces injury has been inconclusive. However, if a joint cannot move freely through the correct ROM, either it, or another joint, will be compromised to achieve it. This results in excessive loading of these joints during sculling and, in some cases, this may cause injury.

Stretching is often the first thing that is overlooked on an athlete's programme, or it is forgotten in the rush from getting out of bed in the morning to getting on the water. It is important to take 10–15min before and after training to stretch. There are many stretching techniques that range from the simple push and stretch to the elaborate partner-assisted proprioceptive neuromuscular facilitation. All fall into two categories: passive and active.

Passive stretching can be defined as something or someone other than the athlete creating the stretching movement, although the athlete may be active during the stretch. Weights, gravity, machines or another person may be used to stretch a joint further than if these outside influences were not applied. Passive stretching can occur when you first start sculling as you stretch with the momentum of the boat and the increasing stroke length.

Active stretching is to stretch to a point of discomfort before relaxing. Here, the muscles are actively stretching the body beyond the ROM.

Stretching is quite safe as long as it is undertaken with a degree of caution, especially when the ROM is being pushed further than a little discomfort. Stretching should be done before and after training sessions. Although a general stretching programme is satisfactory to begin with, as you become more established you should consult your coach and a physiotherapist for a more individualized programme.

Warm-up stretching increases the ROM for the session and can allow for better skill application during the session. Stretching should be preceded by 5min of light aerobic activity that will slightly elevate the body's temperature allowing better blood flow to the muscles, which will allow more effective stretching. The purpose of warm-up stretching is as a preparation for the training session; it does not enhance flexibility.

Stretching after exercise has two benefits. First, it will stretch out any muscles and joints that have become tight during a sculling session. These are generally the hips, hamstrings and shoulders. Second, stretching after training, when the body's temperature has been elevated for an extended period and the muscles are at their most elastic, further increases ROM and will enhance your long-term flexibility.

The following is a general stretching programme. Each stretch should be held for 20–30s.

HIP-FLEXOR STRETCH

Your non-active leg is in front of you with the knee at 90 degrees. Your stretching leg is back as far as it will go. Make sure your trunk maintains an upright position as you push through and feel the stretch over the top of each hip.

HAMSTRING STRETCH

Lying on your back, bring your stretching leg up to your chest and straighten while grasping

---

Stretching

- Aerobic activity for 5min should be done prior to stretching.
- Stretch for 10–15min before and after training.
- Stretch to a point of mild discomfort.
- Breathing should be controlled and rhythmical.
- Hold the stretch for 20–30s.

The hip-flexor stretch.

LEFT: The hamstring stretch.

RIGHT: The groin stretch.

LEFT: The quadricep stretch

RIGHT: The buttock stretch.

your ankles. Draw your leg to your chest with your hands. Bend your non-active leg and maintain good back posture while stretching. You should feel this stretch in the middle of the hamstrings.

QUADRICEP STRETCH

While maintaining good back posture, kneel on one knee and grasp your other ankle with your hands behind you. Your non-active leg is in front of you with your knee at 90 degrees.

Draw your ankle to your buttock and feel the stretch through the quadricep muscles.

GROIN STRETCH

Sit with good posture and with the soles of your shoes touching each other. While holding your feet, press down with your knees and feel the stretch through your groin and inner thigh.

BUTTOCK STRETCH

Lie on your back with the foot of your stretching leg at 90 degrees to your trunk and with your ankle resting across the thigh of the bent, non-active leg. Push out your knee with your elbow and feel the stretch through the gluteal muscles.

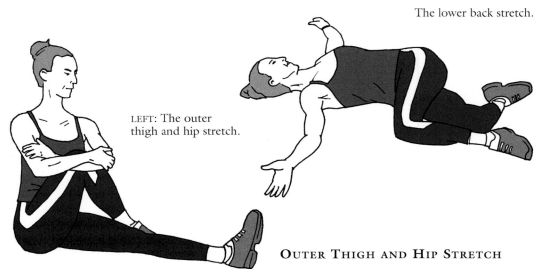

The lower back stretch.

LEFT: The outer thigh and hip stretch.

The shoulder stretch.

OUTER THIGH AND HIP STRETCH

Sit with good back posture and the non-active leg straight out in front of you. Bring the stretching leg over the non-active leg with your foot on the outside of your knee. Draw your knee to your chest and feel the stretch through the outside of the quadriceps and through your hips.

LOWER BACK STRETCH

Lie on your back with your arms out to the side and the non-active leg bent. Roll your stretching leg over the non-active leg at 90 degrees to your trunk. You can either pull down on the stretching leg or leave it to gravity. Try to keep your shoulders and arms on the floor, you will feel the stretch through your lower back.

SHOULDER STRETCH

Standing straight with good posture, put both hands above your head. Keeping your elbows high, place the stretching arm's hand behind your back. Take the hand of the non-active arm and place it on the stretching arm's elbow. Use your hand to draw down on your elbow and feel the stretch through your shoulder.

FOREARM STRETCH

Stand with good posture, your arms out with hands extended. Place your non-active hand on the fingers of your outstretched fingers. Drawing back on your fingers, feel the stretch through your forearms.

LATISSIMUS DORSI STRETCH

Kneel with your thighs at 90 degrees to the floor, your outstretched arms face up, as the other point of contact with the floor. Draw down and feel the stretch through the latissimus dorsi muscle below your shoulder blades.

TESTING

A vital component in assessing and reviewing the training programme is selecting the most appropriate tests that indicate improvement or regression of your training adaptations. As the body adapts to the training stimuli, you will need to assess whether another type of training modality or an increase in volume will take you to a higher level of fitness and boat speed. To get the most out of training, you have to understand the objective of every session, the training to be monitored, and that the period of training should always be assessed. The monitoring and assessment tools used to track progress will be determined by the access you have to sports-science service providers, often universities or sports institutes. If you cannot access such facilities, there are some very effective field tests that can provide valuable feedback.

It is very easy to fall into the trap of over-testing and so lose a lot of valuable training time in the process. Testing sessions should be scheduled into your training programme during the planning stage. It should be reliable, specific, repeatable, accurate and standardized. Often this will require a pre-test protocol prior to testing. If, for example, lactate analysis is part of the testing protocol, doing weights the day before the test may affect the reliability of the lactate samples.

The forearm stretch.

The latissimus dorsi stretch.

Standard on-water tests

Preparation phase testing assessment aims:
- distance/stroke;
- base endurance capacity.

Piece	Workout	Target gold standard (%)
	3 × 2,000m	
1	Rate 20/22 each 1,000m	79
2	Rate 22/24 each 1,000m	82.5
3	Rate 24/26 each 1,000m	86
	1 × 5,000m	
1	Rate 22	81
	1 × 5,000m	
1	Rate 24	84.5
	1 × 5,000m	
	Open rating	90

Pre-competition phase testing assessment aims:
- maintaining distance/stroke as rates move higher;
- anaerobic-threshold development.

Piece	Workout	Target gold standard (%)
	3 × 2,000m	
1	Rate 22/24 each 1,000m	82.5
2	Rate 20/22/24/26 each 500m	84
3	Rate 22/24/26/28 each 500m	86
	1 × 3,000m	
1	Rate 24	81
	1 × 3,000m	
1	Rate 26	87.5
	1 × 3,000m	
1	Open rating	90

Standard on-water tests *(continued)*

Competition phase testing assessment aims:
- consolidating distance/stroke between rates 22 and 30 strokes/min;
- specific-race practice.

Piece	Workout	Target gold standard (%)
	2 × 2,000m	
1	Rate 22/24/26/28 each 500m	86
2	Rate 24/26/28/30 each 500m	88
	3 × 2,000m	
1	Rate 24 500m / Rate 22 1,000m / Rate 24 500m	82.5
2	Rate 26 500m / Rate 24 1,000m / Rate 26 500m	86
3	Rate 28 500m / Rate 26 1,000m / Rate 28 500m	89
	1 × 1,500m + 1 × 500m	
1	1 × 1,500m – racing start – open stroke rate	100
2	1 × 500m – running start – open stroke rate	105
	2 × 500m + 1 × 1,000m	
1	1 × 500m – racing start – open stroke rate	105
2	1 × 1,000m – running start – open stroke rate	102.5
3	1 × 500m – running start – open stroke rate	105

Testing on Water

On-water testing should be a regular part of the training programme and some form of on-water assessment should be made every week. Assessments on the water should always measure your speed against your rate. This will promote power or distance per stroke. As water temperature, stream and wind all affect the conditions under which assessment takes place, the coach should also record the times using a percentage time against the sculler's gold standard time. This will allow for a comparison with a target gold standard time and a comparison between scullers and crews that have been doing the same session, even if they are in different boat classes. Headwinds tend to slow down a sculling or rowing boat more than a tailwind makes it go faster. Therefore, if traffic rules allow, the assessment should always be in still or tailwind conditions. This will provide the most consistent conditions for analysis.

Boat speed and rate should always be analysed together and reflect an increase in rating from the preparation to competition phases. During the competition phase, the on-water

Seat racing for crew selection				
Race distance 1,250m	*Race 1*		*Race 2*	
	Crew	*Crew*	*Crew*	*Crew*
Scullers	A	E	A	E
	B	F	B	F
	C	G	G	C
	D	H	D	H
Race time	3:44.9	3:47.8	3:45.8	3:46.4
Margin		+2.9		+.6
Sculler C beats sculler G by 2.3s				

tests should be race-specific and there should be a mix of tests from a standing start, as well as building from a boat on the run, to test scullers' sprint to the line. The sculler should be executing and analysing race strategy and rhythm during these pieces.

Testing for Selection

Selection of a single sculler is usually straightforward. There is a nominated race or event and the winner takes all. Selection for a crew boat is a little more complicated and can be done in a variety of ways. However, the two main selection methods for crew sculling are seat racing and a sculling matrix.

Seat racing will see two crews racing each other side by side in either a double or quad scull. The most common distances are between 1,250m and 1,750m. These distances are long enough to test scullers' fitness, as well as the boat's moving ability.

At the completion of the first race, two scullers are swapped and the crews race again. The margins of the two races are added and the sculler with the smallest margin will have beaten the other by that margin. This process continues until there is a rank order of eight

scullers. The top four would be selected into the crew. Often the top two or three scullers will be selected into the quad from their single sculling performances and there will be a race for the last seat. For the integrity of the assessment process it is good practice that the scullers do not know who is being seat-raced. A below-par performance may be manipulated by one of the crew members that can affect somebody else's result.

The sculling matrix provides an objective method of assessment. The sculling matrix is usually done using double sculls. It provides the coach or selectors with a rank order of their scullers. The matrix is done in a time-trial format so that the scullers are unaware of their position during the trial. This means all scullers will be racing at their maximum capacity. As with seat-racing, matrices are raced over distances between 1,250m and 1,750m. The eight scullers that participated in the quads seat-racing would matrix in four doubles. Each sculler has the opportunity to race with each of the others during the matrix series. At the end of each race the total times of a sculler's races are added up. The sculler with the least amount of accumulated time is the winner and the accumulated times from the least to

Results of a sculling matrix system

RACE 1

Bow	Stroke	Time
A	E	5:12.0
B	F	5:13.5
C	G	5:13.0
D	H	5:25.5

RACE 2

Bow	Stroke	Time
B	E	5:12.3
C	F	5:14.4
D	G	5:12.6
A	H	5:17.6

RACE 3

Bow	Stroke	Time
C	E	5:15.5
D	F	5:20.6
A	G	5:17.4
B	H	5:15.3

RACE 4

Bow	Stroke	Time
D	E	5:16.5
A	F	5:21.3
B	G	5:16.0

C	H	5:18.6

RACE 5

Bow	Stroke	Time
A	B	5:16.7
C	D	5:18.6
E	F	5:14.8
G	H	5:19.8

RACE 6

Bow	Stroke	Time
A	C	5:23.0
B	D	5:12.7
E	G	5:15.4
F	H	5:15.3

RACE 7

Bow	Stroke	Time
A	D	5:14.5
B	C	5:16.5
E	H	5:18.4
F	G	5:17.6

greatest, provide the rank order for the competitors.

The benefits of the matrix are that it is very objective and everybody gets to scull with everybody else. It is in a time-trial format with approximately 15s between each crew. As nobody knows their position, there is little opportunity for the results to be manipulated. Seat-racing has the greater chance to be manipulated, as the sculler's position is a lot clearer because the crews race side by side. However, due to seat-racing being raced with crews side by side, the sculler is being tested under race-specific stress. This allows the

Accumulative results matrix

Sculler	Accumulative time	Rank
B	36:43.0	1
E	36:44.9	2
G	36:51.8	3
F	36:57.5	4
C	36:59.6	5
D	37:01.0	6
A	37:02.5	7
H	37:10.5	8

sculler's competitive character to be displayed during the racing. Both seat-racing and the matrix method can be done with rating caps to reflect the sculler's training intensity in out of competition phases.

Testing on the Ergometer

Most rowing and sculling programmes involve ergometer training and testing. Ergometer testing can provide objective data about fitness levels, technical ability and mental toughness. It should be the tool around which coaches base their testing battery.

The most commonly used and reliable ergometer is the *Concept 2*. The latest D model has a force curve profile and downloading facility, so that workouts and tests can be downloaded directly to a lap-top computer.

This type of ergometer has a chain moving around a stationary flywheel to offer resistance to the athlete. Other ergometers are available that also provide resistance through water. The *Rowperfect* has the handle, seat and a flywheel that is connected to the moving feet, which is a useful tool when analysing rowing technique. The action of the moving seat and feet is similar to that of a boat, allowing you to practise your pick up at the beginning of the stroke. The *Rowperfect* also provide force profiles and the facility to download to a computer.

As scullers can range from a 55kg lightweight woman to a 100kg heavyweight man, the resistance against the flywheel has to be adjusted to a level similar to that experienced on the water. On the *Concept 2* ergometer, this adjustment is made by altering a damper on the side, which will set the drag factor.

The ergometer can provide force profile feedback with the aid of a lap-top, as well as more rudimentary but nevertheless, effective visual feedback with the use of a mirror.

Recommended drag factors for the *Concept 2* ergometer	
Category	*Drag factor setting*
Junior to senior lightweight women	125
Junior to senior open women	130
Junior to senior lightweight men	135
Junior to senior open men	140

Ergometer testing should test the parameters that are important in sculling performance. The more that coaches plan testing as part of their regular training pattern, the closer the testing will reflect the sculler's level of fitness and ability. There are a number of laboratory-based tests to assess fitness level. These tests usually involve an incremental step test, which provides feedback on the physiological response to a set workload. The incremental step test can be utilized as a sub-maximal test to measure aerobic endurance capacity. Alternatively, a maximum step can be added at the end of the last sub-maximal step to make the test a performance rather than a monitoring test.

Institutions and physiologists use a range of protocols. Generally, most steps have a 4min duration and increment in 25W steps. Heart rates and lactates are measured and graphed against the workload to display a curve representing the response to the workload. If the curve shifts to the right, less of a physiological effort was required to attain the same workload, which indicates an improvement in fitness. If the curve shifts to the left, the opposite is true and the training programme should be

reviewed. If testing in the laboratory, oxygen uptake can also be measured during this type of test. This determines the amount of oxygen you can use from the air you breathe.

The illustration (*below*) shows a successful adaptation to training. Both the lactate and heart rate curves have made a shift to the right indicating less physiological effort for the same workload.

A similar profile can be produced without using the sports-science laboratory. By selecting different standard workloads on the ergometer, a power profile can be produced that indicates which energy zone should be targeted for improvement. By selecting a series of ergometer tests ranging from a sprint to an endurance piece, the results can be overlaid and provide quite a reliable tool to assess progress. This type of testing has the advantage that it may be undertaken without disrupting normal training.

In the power profiles illustrated (*see* p.112), sculler A is exceptionally fit and powerful. She has produced nearly 600W in the 250m test (test 1) and 380W in the 2,000m test (test 2). She has a strong anaerobic threshold with 265W of power for the 30min test (test 3) and

INCREMENTAL STEP TEST

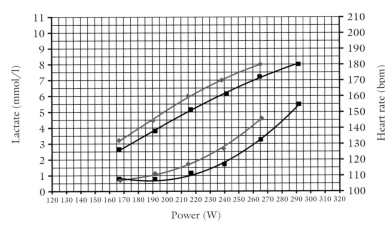

- Lac February 05
- Lac November 04
- HR February 05
- HR November 04

A classic training adaptation shift.

Ergometer tests

Power-profile test battery	Ergometer test distance	Rationale
Test 1	250m	Specific-race sprint.
Test 2	2,000m	Specific-race distance.
Test 3	30min, rate 20	Above anaerobic threshold piece. Rating 20 emphasizes power per stroke.
Test 4	18,000m rate 18 (3 × 6,000m with 90s break for hydration and stretching). For less-trained athletes, it may be appropriate to adjust the distance to 2 × 6,000m.	Base-endurance capacity. Rating 18 emphasizes power per stroke.

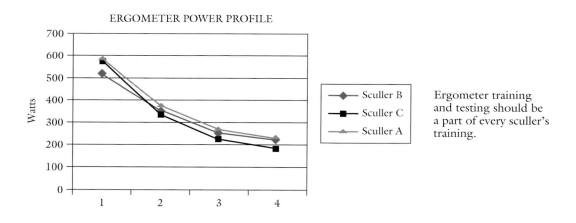

ERGOMETER POWER PROFILE

Ergometer training and testing should be a part of every sculler's training.

a good endurance base producing 225W for the 18,000m test (test 4). Sculler B has a good aerobic base, but as the testing distances become shorter she cannot produce enough power to maintain her curve. This sculler should review her weight and power training. Sculler C demonstrates the opposite; she is very powerful but lacks the endurance to maintain it. She should review her endurance training and intensity. The power profile can be weight-adjusted to suit lightweights. Watts divided by body weight will also provide an effective weight-adjusted profile graph.

Pure power can also be measured on the ergometer with a test where the average watts produced over the ten strokes can be measured.

Testing in the Gym

Scullers and rowers often have dubious weight-lifting techniques. By lifting excessive weights in a test situation, the athletes will over-extend

Exercises that can be considered for testing in the gym

Test	Rationale
Power clean	A similar drive action to the sculling stroke.
Squat	Develops and tests the quadriceps and gluteal muscles, which are important in sculling.
Bench pull	Specific to the arm action of the sculling drive, if the body and chest are kept on the bench during the lift.
Leg press	Good alternative to the squat, if the sculler lacks good squat technique.
Bench press	Develops shoulders, arms and upper-body strength. Make sure that this exercise is always supervised by a safety spotter.
Chin-up	Develops upper-body strength, including shoulders and latissimus dorsi muscle.

their capacity and increase the risk of injury. Testing on machines can reduce this risk.

Traditionally, one and three repetition maximum tests are used to test strength and progress. However, increasing the number of repetitions reduces the amount of weight lifted in a single lift and places a technical component to the test that also assists in preventing a high risk of injury. The table (*above*) shows a series of exercises that can be considered for testing.

When selecting which strength exercises to test, it is important to take the sculler's weight-lifting experience and technical ability into consideration. A sample test protocol can be found in Appendix III.

Strength testing can also be done in the laboratory. Due to the extension component of the sculling and rowing stroke, imbalances can develop between the abdomen and hips (flexion) and the hips and back (extension). This may not only lead to injury, but it can also compromise the sculler from getting into the most effective drive position. The absolute strength of the sculler in flexion and extension can be measured, providing a flexion/extension ratio. This type of testing can be done with the legs and the trunk.

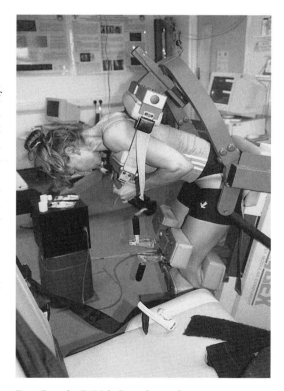

Bev Gough, British Squad member, trunk strength testing at Imperial College, London.

CHAPTER 8
Mental Skills and Racing Strategies

'I felt like I was out of the boat watching it from outside,' said Peter Antonie about his race in Barcelona, when he became Olympic champion. 'I was in the zone, it was like watching a movie. I could see myself, as well as the others. I could feel everything but nothing,' remarked Haining about his victory at the 1993 World Championship. Both these athletes are describing their mental concentration and the sophistication of their mental skills, while under the most extreme pressure of international sport at its highest level.

Whilst writing I have been asking a broad section of the international rowing community what is the best sculling race they have ever seen. Time after time, one race has been mentioned: the final of the men's single-scull at the 1984 Los Angeles Olympics. The two leading scullers of the day were pitted against each other, the fast-starting German, Peter-Michael Kolbe, and the even-paced Finn, Pertti Karppinen. Kris Korzenowski, a world-renowned rowing coach, described this as his most memorable race. There is a stunning photograph of the moment when Karppinen has ranged up next to Kolbe. Both men have their heads turned and are staring at each other. Kris ponders on the psychology of singles racing, 'Looking at each other these guys know this is the moment, they both knew one was to win and the other to lose. You can put yourself in their position – what goes through their minds? Or is it just racing instinct?' (Karppinen sculled away from Kolbe to become the champion.)

Is it just instinct, as Korzenowski pondered, or is there a set of skills that can be developed? One thing is certain, there are a series of mental skills that you can develop to maximize your potential, whether racing for Olympic glory or at club level. These skills need to be rehearsed daily during training and refined for racing. Mental skills should have the same priority as physiological improvements and technical gains in a training programme.

The following section aims to provide you with an overview of some mental skills that may assist you in improving your sculling. Four fundamental skills that help to improve performance are: goal setting; race planning; visualization; and maintaining a training diary.

GOAL SETTING

There are two types of goals: outcome and process. Outcome goals refer to the outcome of the result you desire, for example, to win a championship. Process goals refer to specific tasks that have to be applied to achieve the desired outcome. Process goals are smaller and more specific than outcome goals. When achieved, process goals will provide you with the opportunity to attain the outcome goal. For example, achievement of a goal to place your blades in the water before you drive your legs, results in you rowing faster and more effectively, moving you closer to attaining your ultimate goal. Goal setting requires a significant amount of thought and planning. All too often goals are set, written down and then put in a bottom drawer and forgotten about, until next season.

Starting in the off-season, you need to ask yourself the following questions:

• What is the season's aim?
• What is required to achieve this aim?
• What do I need to do to meet these requirements?

Once the initial goals have been set, you need to review progress towards the goals on a regular basis; reassess how realistic the goals are and set goals for the next period. If the aim is to win the final of the Diamond Sculls at the Henley Royal Regatta, the following performance standards would have to be met. Just to reach the final, you will need to achieve an extremely high standard. To win, you will need to be capable of doing a 2,000m race under

6min 55s. To achieve this, the following parameters must be attained:

• U2 training speed at rate 18: 2min 12s to 2min 17s;
• 2,000m rate 28: <7min 24s;
• 1,000m time at racing: <3min 18s;
• 500m time at racing: <1min 34s;
• 2,000m ergometer score: <6min 0s;
• power clean: 100kg;
• back squat: 110kg;
• stroke length: 110 degrees.

You then need to assess your current level of performance at these parameters and know by how much you have to improve. You then have to ascertain what actions you are required to do to improve your level of performance. It is important to set a time-frame for change.

The expression 'a giant staircase can be climbed by taking one step at a time' is

---

Sample goal-setting matrix

AIM: To race in final of the Diamond Sculls at Henley Royal Regatta

Performance parameter	Outcome goal task	Current level of task	Deficit	Process action to improve	Review
2,000m race					
Time = 6min 55s	Rate 18 U2 speed = 2min 12s–2min 17s/500m	Average U2 speed = 2min 16s/500m	+4s/500m	Blade accuracy at front turn	Weekly with video
	2,000m rate 28 time = 7min 24s (92.7%)	Best time = 7min 29s	+5s	Even split through middle-two 500m	2,000m measured piece fortnightly. Split time to review even pace.

(*continued overleaf*)

Sample goal-setting matrix *(continued)*

Performance parameter	Outcome goal task	Current level of task	Deficit	Process action to improve	Review
	1,000m race piece <3min 18s	Best time = 3:20.5 average rate 33 strokes per minute	+2.5s	Improve leg/back drive co-ordination to increase rate to 35 strokes/min	Video and review rate profile
	500m race piece <1min 34s	Best time = 1min 34.5s	+5s	Come out to full length earlier after start	Video
	2,000m ergometer score <6min 0s	Best score = 6min 04.3s Rate 30	+4.3s	Improve length through better rock-over. Supplementary stretching and trunk-strengthening exercises.	Review at each ergometer workout
	Power clean 100kg	Personal best = 96.4kg	−3.6kg	Greater drive through hips and shrug	Technical focus and review during all weights + video
	Back squat 110kg	Personal best = 105kg	Back position collapses during drive	Supplementary trunk-strengthening exercises	Technical focus and review during all weights + video
	Sculling stroke length = 110 degrees	Currently 105 degrees	−5 degrees	Improve rock-over from finish position. Activate gluteal and lower abdominal muscles throughout the finish of the stroke.	Video and review weekly

extremely appropriate to sculling and rowing. You need a clear understanding of the aim of each training session and whether or not you have achieved it. Focusing on the present also

takes care of your long-term results. Before getting on the water, you should have a clear idea of what you are going to do. When you get off, you should know how far you went towards achieving your goal and what you need to do to consolidate it.

Goal-Setting Tips

Concentrate on process goals rather than outcome goals.
Make goals realistic but challenging.
Review regularly.
Reset when appropriate.

RACE PLANNING

Process goals lay the foundation for the race plan. A race plan is a tool to structure your thinking when racing. By dividing the

Sample race plan				
Distance	Call	Think	Do	500m aims
0	'Length' 'Flat'	Build slide length by stroke 7 Only bury blades	Full length Flat draw	Fast start and establish rhythm
250m	'Power rhythm'	Feel for boat and establish rhythm	Focus on pushing legs and feeling the boat's run	
500m	'Legs'	Long leg drive	Drive through hips	Maintain speed and rhythm, and attack
750m	'Long arms'	Lever boat	Straight-arm drive – push do not pull	
1,000m	'Length'	Maintain press-out, rock-over and slide length	Attack with legs and full-slide length	Commit to each stroke and attack
1,250m	'Rhythm'	Feel for the power and the boat's run	Attack – push legs and feel for the boat's run	
1,500m	'Catches'	Accurate front turn	Swing arms out and up faster	Attack – sprint building speed to the finish line
1,750m	'Legs' 'Bodies'	Dynamic leg drive	Drive through hips	
2,000m	'Legs'	Lever boat with body swing Dynamic leg drive	Lever back off legs Drive through hips	

117

2,000m race distance into bite-size pieces, you can develop specific focus points. Usually this means four-500m sections. Each section will have a specific goal to maximize the boat's speed. These can be either tactical or technical and are different for each crew. This provides the crew with cues that will assist them with remaining focused on the job at hand when under the stress of racing.

Pre-competition routines and day plans are useful tools at regattas. However, it is important to establish a pre-competition routine that works for you. This will mean experimenting until you find the right routine that gets you into the optimal racing frame of mind. Early season regattas are ideal for trying or refining different pre-race routines. These routines will include the race warm-up on land and water, visualization, pre-race coaching, crew briefing and de-briefing, and the weigh-in for lightweights.

Planning the day's racing is of utmost importance. Every day of racing, you should write down where, when and how you want to feel through the race day. By sticking to a plan and pre-setting where you want to be in your head, you are maximizing your chances of success. You will be better able to attain your optimal arousal level at race time.

A regatta is a very busy place and an important skill that scullers need to develop is to 'switch on' and 'switch off'. This can be shown in the day plan, where there is time to be focused on racing and other time to get right away from it and relax. There is little point in racing the race before the race! However, there is an extremely useful mental skill that will allow you to rehearse your race – visualization.

VISUALIZATION

Visualization or mental rehearsal is a skill that should be used, developed and practised daily.

Its purpose is to create a picture in your mind of what should be happening – it could be a technical improvement or a race rehearsal. Scullers and crews can develop this skill to the level whereby they can mentally rehearse their race crossing the finish line at the same time as their race actually takes. Both Peter Antonie and Peter Haining, at the beginning of this chapter, were describing the 'zone' they were in. They had rehearsed what they were going to do and during the race they could describe what they were doing and that they had this feeling they were out of the boat watching in.

Scullers should be using all three of their senses when visualizing: you should see yourself sculling; you should be able to picture yourself from where you sit in the boat; and you should be able to see yourself from the side and above. You should be able to feel the sculls in your hands and the pressure being applied on the face of the blades in the water. You should be able to hear the boat moving through the water, your breathing and your self-talk. The most effective visualization will occur after you have relaxed. Finding a quiet and comfortable location for visualization will help, as will doing some relaxation techniques prior to visualizing.

It is important to have a clear picture of what you should look like when sculling and visualizing. Using images from role models is an effective method to imprint the perfect stroke in your mind. Visualization should not just be seen as a race skill but also as an effective training tool. Used often, it will accelerate technical changes.

Visualization Tips

- Start with a relaxation technique.
- See what should be happening.
- Use visual, auditory and kinaesthetic cues.
- Be specific.

TRAINING DIARIES

Every sculler should keep a training diary. It should contain a brief note about each training session and include goals and objectives, details of technical focus and development, training programme and race plans, as well as objective data such as times from pieces on the water, weights lifted and testing data. This information may be used to ascertain what works best for you and also to document your progress throughout the season.

During a sculling season there will always be challenges that will knock your confidence. So be sure to include a list of confidence-builders at the back of the diary. This should contain details of all your achievements, such as race victories and technical breakthroughs. It should be reviewed often and acknowledged. When confidence is falling prior to regattas or when you are nervous, are very good times to sit down and review what you have done well. Confident scullers are fast scullers!

Whether you are competing in the Masters, university, club or elite level, training for competitions is time-consuming. There will always be competing demands on your time, so you must develop good time-management and prioritizing skills to juggle sculling, family, career aspirations, education demands and relationships. Sports psychologists and other professionals can provide help to build up these skills. Other areas where these professionals can help include:

- communication skills;
- assertiveness training;
- conflict resolution;
- group/crew dynamics;
- concentration skills;
- confidence building;
- anxiety control.

Rowing associations, sporting institutions and the Internet are good ways to find a sports psychologist that can help you. There are also many good publications available, some of which appear in the Further Reading list.

RACING STRATEGIES

During the 1970s, the Hansen brothers from Norway dominated men's double-sculling. In 1976, at the Montreal Olympics they won the gold medal in the double scull. Melch Burgin, a sculling Olympic medallist from Switzerland and boat-builder for the famous Stampfli racing boats, has been part of the international rowing scene for the last four decades. He recalls that it was determination that separated the Norwegian crew from the others:

> They were so determined to do it [win] each stroke. With good technique and determination they moved the boat with every stroke.... They always came from behind in the second 1,000m – the second wind – their focus every stroke was on winning the race.

Melch also reflected on his own successful career. In 1966 on Lake Rotsee in Switzerland, Melch raced the legendary Olympic sculling champion Ivanov from the then Soviet Union. Melch recalled that:

> Ivanov was 10cm taller, 20kg heavier and ten times more experienced. I really wanted to beat him. To do it I had to rate 38–40 [strokes/min], he would be at 34. I remember doing my sprints and high rate and every time I pushed, Ivanov always came back; there was a point where I was ready to give up. I was in lane one Ivanov lane two.

As the two scullers passed close to the shore after 1,250m, with Melch about to relinquish the race, he heard a spectator call out: 'One more sprint and you have him!'. 'So I made one more sprint and Ivanov gave up!' Melch did not realize that Ivanov had rowed himself to exhaustion. By the time Melch got back to the boating pontoon, Ivanov was receiving medical assistance and he had to go to hospital. 'I offered to drive him there and he accepted. He went in my car to the hospital!' An example of the respect and camaraderie that sculling and rowing engenders.

Racing strategies relate to the distribution of speed over the entire race. In 2,000m racing, race strategy relates to the speed that can be produced through each of the four 500m sections. Crews may be strong in the first section of the race and fade in the last 500m. Alternatively, as with the Hansen brothers from Norway, the crew may be steady out of the start and finish strongly in the second half of the race. There are many reasons why different strategies are adopted but they will usually reflect the training, physiology, technical ability and mental toughness of the sculler. The quality of the opposition will also be an influencing factor.

Racing tactics refer to the interrelationship between opposing scullers in a race. Melch's race with Ivanov was all about tactics, racing assertively and the element of surprise. Tactics play a greater role than strategy in events such as Henley Royal Regatta, where there are only two crews racing at a time, as opposed to six-lane 2,000m racing.

To control a race you need to make a fast start to get in front, so that you are able to see and match any moves that may come from the opposition. The risky nature of this tactic (often called 'do or die') is that if you sprint too hard from the start, a high level of lactic acid will build up and there is a risk of fatigue or 'blowing up' setting in before the finish line. You must develop a pacing strategy that you have practised in training, so that you are able to execute the most effective race strategy and tactics.

When assessing race strategies, an effective method is to calculate the average speed and review each 500m split time, above or below the average race speed. To compare across boat categories and different weather conditions, the time can be expressed as a percentage above or below the average speed. For example, the table (*below*) shows the race strategy used in the final of the Athens Olympic Games in the women's quad-scull final, where Germany won the gold and Great Britain the silver.

Using this assessment, you can see how the German crew stayed closer to their average speed throughout the second 500m, a strategy that gave them a clear lead. The British crew closed the gap in the second 1,000m and raced much closer to their average speed than the Germans; however, they could not overcome the deficit from the second 500m.

Dr Valery Kleshnev, himself an Olympic sculling medallist, assessed a total of 977 World Cup, World Championship and Olympic races, between 1993 and 2001. During this period,

Race strategy used in the final of the Athens Olympic Games in the women's quad-scull final				
Crew	1st 500m (%)	2nd 500m (%)	3rd 500m (%)	4th 500m (%)
Germany	+2.77	−0.26	−1.29	−1.22
Great Britain	+2.80	−1.27	−0.89	−0.64

winners were found to be faster relative to their average speed in the first section of the race, compared to the silver and bronze medallists, who over the same period were faster in the last section of the race than the gold medallists. The average boat-speed deviation decreased over the period, seeing crews race closer to their average. The boat-speed variation decreased from 2.7 per cent in 1993 to 1.7 per cent in 2001.

These trends have some interesting ramifications for the psychological, technical and physiological preparation for a race. If you make a fast start and a fast first section, you will be in a position to respond and cover the opposition's moves and to press for the win. By winning races this way, you will also 'learn' to win and gain confidence for more difficult races. However, you can only maintain such speed if you are fit and sculling with a good rhythm and technique. Often, although a fast start may be achieved through powerful short strokes and a high rating, the speed cannot be maintained and opponents with a longer and more rhythmical stroke will take the lead. The trend in racing strategy places emphasis on the need for rhythm, as well as power and endurance, in the training programme. Training and preparation also need to provide an environment where you are able to hone your mental skills of pacing and tactics.

There is a difference in strategy between the smaller boats (singles and doubles) and the larger ones (quads). Smaller boats have the ability to accelerate very quickly and tend to reach a higher speed earlier in the race relative to the big boats, which build their momentum and generally have a more consistent speed with less of a drop in the later sections of the race.

These strategy trends are also valid for the two-lane Henley-style regattas. Coach educator Nigel Weare analysed all the races at the 1990 Henley Royal Regatta and found that 215 winning crews from 250 races were leading at the barrier, which is less than 2min from the start. Tactics are even more important for the two-crew boat races, as once the opposition has the ascendancy, it is very tough to come from behind. In some races, once a crew is in front, they can also get a better steering line or, indeed, wash down the losing boat with their scull's puddles.

It is very easy to lose your focus during races. Although it is a natural instinct to focus on whether you are in front or not, it is very important in competitive sculling to keep your mind on your own boat. As much as you might want to, you cannot slow the opposition down! Your focus should be on the processes that maximize your boat speed. The closer the race, the greater your concentration has to be. Kleshnev found that between 1993 and 2001, the average difference in boat speed between the medallists in World Cups, World Championships and the Olympic Games was 0.35 per cent. So every stroke really does count.

CHAPTER 9
Healthy Sculling and Injury Prevention

Sculling and rowing provide many health benefits. Sculling develops a strong musculature and an improved cardiovascular system. It is also a safe sport with low injury rates. This chapter aims to identify some common injuries and illnesses that afflict scullers and provide some tips on how to prevent them. Whenever a sculler presents to training with an injury or illness, a professional medical opinion should always be sought.

The Australian Institute of Sport (AIS) conducted a study of injuries over the first ten years (1985–94) of their scholarship programme (Hickey *et al.*, 1997). They found only a small number of major injuries but quite a few mild and moderate injuries, some of the most frequently encountered being chest-rib stress fractures and lower back injuries. Most injuries were chronic and not acute reflecting the repetitive nature of rowing.

> There are two mistakes people make. A sudden change or increase too quickly in training volume or gearing, and the non-periodization of training lead people to being ill and injured and not reaching their full potential.
>
> **Richard Budgett,**
> *Olympic gold medallist and*
> *British Olympic team doctor*

UPPER RESPIRATORY TRACT INFECTIONS

Other research at the AIS showed that the most prevalent illness amongst the athletes was the common cold (upper respiratory tract infection – URTI). Adults generally have between two and three colds a year. The AIS study showed that athletes in high-level training suffered three colds annually and up to 25 per cent would suffer four or more. It has been suggested that moderate aerobic training can improve the body's immune system, which, in turn, may reduce the chance of contracting a cold. Conversely, high-intensity training has been shown to suppress the immune system. This is of particular concern when the athlete is tapering for an event and the training volume is decreasing while the training intensity is increasing.

There are some simple guidelines that should be followed to reduce the likelihood of contracting a cold. The training programme should always have a component of aerobic training and be well-monitored. Monitoring certain parameters in the morning can give a good indication of the physical and mental state of the sculler, and training can then be adjusted accordingly. The morning is also the best time of the day to check heart rate and body weight, which can also indicate undue stress. In general, if the resting heart rate is up to five beats above an individual's average resting level, normal training may proceed. If the heart rate is five to ten beats above average, then only aerobic training should be prescribed. If the heart rate is more than ten beats above average, then the athlete should be rested.

Body weight is also a good indicator of fatigue. It is very important to maintain a balanced diet. If the diet is normal and consistent, a rapid loss of weight may indicate either dehydration or the sculler being in a state where they are failing to adapt to the training programme. A loss of appetite may also indicate that the sculler is overly fatigued. Monitoring subjective markers, such as the quality of sleep and level of vitality, may also help in assessing the level of fatigue. Psychological stress is also believed to suppress the immune system. Developing coping strategies and having the ability to relax can help you to deal with the stresses of life, training and competition.

It is always good practice to avoid coming in to contact with viruses and bacteria. This is most effectively done by following good general hygiene routines. Even Olympic-level rowers and scullers are schooled in the art of how to wash their hands! Wash your hands regularly, especially after going to the toilet and before meals. Do not forget to wash your thumbs. Keep your hands away from your mouth (especially if they have been in contact with the water) or from wiping your nose. Never share water bottles, towels or other personal items. Avoid handling food – use utensils. Keep your sculling handles clean.

Dressing for weather conditions with warm-and water-resistant clothing during the winter months will provide some protection against succumbing to cold-weather illnesses (you should also consider having a 'flu jab). Wearing hats, sunscreen and appropriate warm-weather clothing can help to avoid sunburn and the long-term effects of sun exposure.

COMMON INJURIES

Stress Fractures of the Rib

Rib stress-fractures in scullers and rowers are an insidious injury. Generally, if rib pain occurs and a hot spot appears on a bone scan, the sculler will be out of the boat for between four and six weeks. Usually, stress fractures in rowers occur in the mid-auxiliary line, which is on the side roughly in line with the armpit; whilst in scullers, studies suggest that they occur more often on the back of the ribcage. This, however, can vary from person to person. Several theories exist about how these fractures occur: some incriminate the anterior serratus muscle, others the oblique. However, to date there is no definitive evidence to account for them. Many clinicians believe it to be related to posture during rowing, with poor postures compromising shoulder girdle function (*see* section on posture and body position during rowing, as well as the section on trunk strengthening).

Whilst it is still unclear what causes rib stress-fractures, it is clear that they have become more prevalent over the last two decades. During this time the construction of sculls has changed from timber to carbon, as well as, more recently, a move to a greater surface area of the blade. This has created a stiffer scull with a stronger connection with the water. This in turn creates a greater force for the sculler to lever, which leads to a greater stress through the sculler's trunk.

It has also been reported that sudden increases in training volume and intensity may make a sculler more susceptible to stress fractures. Changing sides in rowing or moving from sculling to sweep, also may make the rower more susceptible to stress fractures. Consideration for such extrinsic injury mechanisms needs to be considered. However, until more is known about how these injuries occur, preventative strategies are hard to define and defend.

Correct gearing ratios and gradual increases in volume and intensity of training can reduce the risk of stress fractures. Through weight training you can develop general strength through your upper body. This requires your weights programme to develop a balance between the muscles that produce force during the stroke, and the muscles that support and oppose them. Regular review by a physiotherapist and manipulation to prevent the thoracic spine becoming tight, may also assist in preventing rib stress-fractures, along with correct strengthening and stability training for the pelvic and shoulder girdle complexes.

Lower Back Pain

The repetitive nature of sculling, lack of trunk strength and control, together with poor sculling and weight technique, can contribute to lower back pain. This pain can be low-grade, which can be relieved through adjusting training or by resting; or it can be a career-ending prolapsed disc, which requires surgery.

According to national figures, up to 80 per cent of the general population can expect to suffer from back pain at some point in their lives. Consequently, not all back pain can be blamed on sculling. As with rib fractures, the mechanism of the injury is not known. However, current evidence suggests that part of training should involve exercises to address posture and trunk strength. Approximately 30 per cent of power can be produced through the trunk. To be effective in applying that power, the back must be capable of sustaining a strong position.

The nature of sculling technique develops a strong extension of the body's trunk through the drive. The athlete needs to develop the abdominal muscles in order to create a balance between the trunk's flexion (recovery phase) and extension (drive phase). Correct trunk position increases the amount of power that can be produced and helps prevent lower back injuries.

It is important to develop and activate the correct muscles to use the trunk through the stroke. Scullers often use their hip flexors instead of gluteal and lower abdominal muscles, to work the trunk during the stroke. Studies have indicated that there is a strong correlation between over-developed hip flexors and back pain. Over-developed hip flexors tend to pull the trunk forward during the recovery phase of the stroke and give the impression of a rounded back and as such prevent correct use of the pelvis. This is accentuated by a shift in the balance of the back flexors and extensors, and poor endurance of the back muscles in rowers.

To address these issues, you should undertake a trunk-strengthening programme in conjunction with a stretching programme of the hip flexor and hamstring muscles. The trunk strengthening should be sequenced through an awareness stage, where you can identify and activate deep lower abdominal muscles, followed by strength and endurance training. This training should be aimed at the gluteal, oblique and lower abdominal muscles, which provide stability to the back and pelvis. It should focus on endurance, as well as strength. An example of a trunk-strengthening programme will be found in Chapter 7.

Often weights training can be incriminated with respect to causing back problems. This is generally due to poor weight-lifting technique. You should be as focused on improving your weight-lifting technique as you are with your sculling technique.

However, if unremitting back pain or shooting pain down the leg is experienced, a health professional should be contacted immediately.

Blisters

Blisters on the hands are the occupational hazard of all those who sit on the water with sculls or oars in their hands. Hands toughen as the miles increase, but a few weeks rest can leave the hands red and raw when the sculler returns to the water. The blister forms through friction between the hand and the scull's handles. A change of handles or the scull's grip can be enough to irritate the hands. Once the blister forms, it is painful and, if it breaks, has the potential to become infected. This is why handles should be cleaned regularly with soap and water and, occasionally, with disinfectant.

In the first instance, reducing rowing time is often enough to reduce the pressure on the hands and relieve the symptoms. Once a blister is formed, and/or breaks, it is best to keep the blister's skin intact to offer a barrier to the raw skin under the blister. If it breaks, it is important to keep the hands clean with soap and water or antiseptic solutions to prevent infection. If the site where the blister is on the hand deteriorates further, cracks can form that are extremely painful. Filling the crack with 'skin glue' can assist in sealing the crack and assist in the healing process, as well as provide some pain relief. Once a callus has formed on the hand, it should be kept trimmed or sanded down to prevent blisters from forming underneath.

NUTRITION

Much time and effort is spent on training, rigging of the boat and improving technique. To maximize these efforts on the water and in the gym, the body must be provided with the correct fuel. The human physiological system is similar to the working system of a machine. The body needs fuel to produce energy that in turn operates its different physiological systems.

There is an optimum amount and type of fuel required to achieve the high levels of energy production needed for rowing. The highly tuned formula one racing car is not fuelled with lead replacement petrol. You should assess what you eat and optimize your fuel intake in order to optimize your performance. For the serious sculler, it is worthwhile accessing a sports nutritionist to analyse, review and guide your dietary intake. Recording your eating habits through a diet diary can be an effective way of analysing your diet. By working through a nutritionist, the advice you get should be sound and based on science, rather than the many myths that surround eating and sport.

A Balanced Diet

A well-balanced diet of good quality food will maximize the benefits of training. The majority of the dietary intake should be in the form of carbohydrate, which contributes to the glycogen energy stores in the body's muscles. There are two types of carbohydrates: simple and complex. Simple carbohydrates are sugars with small amounts of nutrients, typically found in sugar, honey and sweet foods. Complex carbohydrates are rich in nutrients and are found in wholemeal breads, wholemeal pasta, potatoes, rice and breakfast cereals. Approximately half of the diet should be made up of complex carbohydrates. Fresh fruit and vegetables, fruit juices and legumes are also good sources of carbohydrate and are also a source of protein, fibre, vitamins and minerals. Regular but not necessary large servings of animal flesh and vegetarian alternatives, as well as dairy products, are good sources for protein, iron and calcium.

You should be aiming for a low-fat rather than a no-fat diet, as fats contain essential fat-soluble vitamins. Saturated fats come from animals, are high in calories, but do contain fat-soluble vitamins. Eating a low-fat diet will help to control body weight. Unsaturated fats contain fat-soluble vitamins and anti-oxidants that may have some beneficial health and recovery value. Unsaturated fats are in margarine, nuts, seeds and olive oil, and should be taken in small servings.

Diet and Training

Training often takes place early in the morning or after study or work in the afternoon. It is important, therefore, to plan your eating well. If food is not consumed prior to the morning training session, and your last meal was during the previous evening, then your glycogen stores will be low before starting training and, consequently, the quality of your training will be compromised. Glycogen depletion will cause the body to utilize fat as an energy store. Fat takes a longer time to convert to energy and requires more oxygen for the energy-conversion process, than does glycogen. If you are training in the evening and miss lunch, then you will be in a similar position and, again, your training will be compromised. It is important for you to plan your meals so that you can get the best quality training and maximize the benefits from your training.

A light snack of some bread or toast before the morning training session will be enough to provide carbohydrate for effective training. The snack should be small enough so that it does not repeat during training. A second breakfast after the morning training will replace glycogen lost during the session. Lunch should be as normal, but a small snack before the afternoon training session will again bolster your carbohydrate stores in preparation for training. Dinner will replenish depleted glycogen stores from the afternoon's training.

Heavyweight male scullers can eat up to 6,000 calories a day to provide their bodies with enough fuel to handle large training volumes. Lightweights, conversely, may eat between 1,500 and 2,000 calories a day to avoid weight gain or to lose weight. It is important for performance that these calories are consumed from nutrient-rich foods in a well-balanced diet. When eating carbohydrate after training to refuel glycogen stores, aim to eat 1–2g of carbohydrate per kg of body weight within the first 2h after training.

Drinking a weak carbohydrate drink during training will help maintain glycogen stores through long training sessions and may enhance the body's immune function. For maximum digestion of the carbohydrate, the drink should have only approximately 5 per cent carbohydrate. There are now available many commercial sports drinks and supplement food bars. Make sure you use the drink that is right for your training needs and taste.

During the taper phase of training into the regatta, the amount of training volume will be reduced and you will not require as many calories to meet your energy demands. Therefore, you should adjust the amount of food you are consuming. Your diet should maintain a high percentage of carbohydrate, as well as some protein and plenty of fluids. Generally, large meals should not be consumed within 4h of racing, and light meals up to 90min prior to racing. When exercising, blood moves from the stomach into the exercising muscles. This can cause discomfort if there is undigested food in the stomach. Meal-replacement products are available for scullers who suffer from pre-race stomach nerves. As with all parts of racing, your pre-racing meal plan should be rehearsed and adjusted until you find the most effective method and foods.

HYDRATION

During sculling the body heats up and sweating is the predominant mechanism that the body uses to cool down. During a training session in warm weather, up to 2ltr of water a day can be lost through sweating. Dehydration affects performance – it causes increased stress on the heart and can lead to symptoms of heat stress and illness. Thirst is the body's mechanism to counter dehydration; however, if you are feeling thirsty, then you are already dehydrated to a level that will affect your performance. Therefore, thirst is not a good indicator of dehydration. Dehydration can occur during the cold winter months and scullers are particularly at risk through the winter, as often they do not realize they are dehydrating. The sculler wearing many layers of winter clothes will also sweat a lot during training.

To re-hydrate during training, you should drink often and with small mouthfuls. Make sure you arrive at training hydrated and it is good practice to weigh yourself before and after training. A litre of sweat will weigh a kilogram. A litre of water should be drunk for each kilogram lost during training. When multiple training sessions are taking place throughout the day, you should always be the same weight as you were prior to the first training session before commencing subsequent sessions.

CHAPTER 10
Effective Learning and Coaching

A coach has to fill many roles. Aside from having an astute technical eye, the coach is also a trainer, tactician, communicator, confidant, disciplinarian, instructor, manager, motivator, administrator – and, on occasions, a mind-reader! Most successful coaches have the ability to solve problems. Regardless of the type of problem, a coach needs to be able to analyse a situation, to provide a series of alternatives, to select the most appropriate action, to implement the action and review its effectiveness. Coaches have to be very good at goal setting.

The ability to organize and prioritize are traits that coaches must also have in abundance. To write, implement and review a training programme, to organize training facilities, to transport and rig boats, as well as oversee athletes on a daily basis, often requires more hours than there are in the day. Prioritizing is another quality trait that successful coaches display.

A good coach will need to spend a great deal of time involved in preparing training sessions, and selecting the most effective training content and instruction method, so that the time available with the athletes is used to the best effect. Good observation and communication skills are also important, in order to provide guidance and feedback, and to be able to present complicated tasks in simple steps.

Learning a new skill is usually undertaken through a four-step process:

- Introduction.
- Demonstration and understanding.
- Practice.
- Review and feedback.

Coaches can complicate and confuse the implementation of a new skill. Often it is best to demonstrate with visual aids and description, then allow the sculler to get on with doing it. Practice and focus are needed to make a new skill an automatic part of the sculler's technique. At first, the skill movements and instructions have to be simple, as scullers learn the gross motor components of the new skill. As they become more confident with the change, they will start to move into the consolidation phase, where they know when they are performing the new skill correctly, but lack consistency. At this stage, scullers often display the new skill and then lose it and are unable to regain it without coaching intervention. The next stage is consistency, which is where scullers can consistently display the new skill and reproduce it at higher stroke rates and intensities.

Remember that athletes, like everyone else, have preferred learning styles. Some individuals learn well visually, some verbally and others through movement or kinaesthetically (feel). Try different approaches to see what works best. Even if someone does not know their own learning style, they can often give you clues in their language. For example, 'I hear what you are saying, that sounds good to me', would be an indication that they learn well verbally. Whereas, 'I can see what you mean, I have a clear vision of what you are asking me to do'

Good coaches are:

- encouraging;
- organized;
- punctual;
- communicators;
- open to new ideas and solutions.

suggests that visual learning might be more appropriate.

Although the learning process can be frustrating, coaches have to be patient and persistent – people will develop through these learning stages at various rates.

The coach–athlete relationship is a partnership. The coach should always understand that the coaching role is to act in the best interests of the athlete. The most productive relationships are based on mutual trust and respect. The coach will not be at the start line with the sculler, so scullers must be taught to be independent and make the correct decisions when they are out on the water in competition. Earlier in this book, Peter Haining described how his coach had rehearsed with him a plan 'B' if anything went wrong during his preparation for the 1993 World Championships:

> When I caught the buoy I went straight to my plan B strategy which I had worked on with my coach, Miles Forbes-Thomas. During training Miles had me doing seven-minute workouts on the leg press machine in the gym. He would suddenly jump on the weights and stop me. You've caught a buoy what are you going to do? When I caught the buoy I had rehearsed the situation over and over – I went ballistic! I had to win…

A good coach also plans for the unexpected.

It is important that the athlete–coach relationship is a two-way concern. Athletes have to engage, to challenge and to get the best out of their coach. If they do this, they are getting the best for themselves.

It is important that coaches do not abuse their position in the coach–athlete relationship.

The Amateur Rowing Association utilizes a code of ethics and conduct for sports coaches. All coaches and rowing clubs should be aware and follow them, especially coaches of children. The code of ethics conduct expects coaches to conform to ethical standards in humanity, relationships, commitment, co-operation, integrity, advertising, confidentiality, abuse of privilege and personal standards. Coaches also have a responsibility to the safety of their charges. Safety, competencies, public criticism of colleagues, misrepresentation, confidentiality, criminal conviction and personal misconduct, are all areas covered by the code of conduct. Coaches need to ensure that they know how to risk-assess and to constantly assess the situation for safety.

One of the most difficult jobs for the coach is to show good leadership under regatta pressure. This is particularly the case if the sculler or crew has under-performed in the preliminary races. Athletes will pick up the coach's body language. When the athlete is at his most nervous and doubting, the coach, who may be feeling the same way, has to put on a brave face and lead from the front. Coaches need to analyse the performance and offer realistic and achievable solutions. The quality of a coach is not seen when crews are riding a wave of optimism but rather when they have suffered a set-back and the coach leads them out of it.

The ARA is currently producing a series of online training resources to support the coach and the self-coached on a wide range of topics. These can be accessed via the ARA website (www.ara-rowing.org).

CHAPTER 11
Sculling Boats and Equipment

BOATS

Most rowing clubs purchase crew boats that provide the highest number of rowing and sculling seats to the greatest number of members. Sculls are generally available for beginners and are usually well-worn. When you arrive at a level of proficiency where the boat becomes a limiting factor to your performance, you should upgrade it. This will probably mean having to buy your own. A new single-sculling boat will cost approximately £3,000; however, there are often very good quality second-hand boats available.

When deciding whether to buy a new or used boat, you should think about the following factors:

- hull shape and size;
- construction method and materials;
- quality;
- a boat-builder's reputation for reliability and after-sales service.

There are many rowing websites and magazines that advertise boats and accessories. With some time spent on research, there are some very good deals available.

Hull Shape and Size

There are many points to consider when selecting a hull shape. The hull is long and narrow to counter the inefficient impulse and run motion of the boat during the drive and recovery phase of the stroke. The water's drag on the hull contributes the majority of the resistance against the boat during the stroke. Reducing the wetted surface area will reduce this drag.

When ordering a boat, the boat-builder will ask what the average weight of the crew is. This is because boat-builders work to a formula that stipulates that the height of the deck should be raised by 1cm from the water for every extra 10kg of average crew weight. If the boat ordered is too small, the gunwales will be too shallow; you will be too close to the water and will find rough water uncomfortable. If the boat is too big, you will feel too high up in it and there will be too much freeboard, which will create unnecessary wind resistance. However, when purchasing a boat it is better to buy one that is slightly too large rather than too small. The rig can be adjusted down and you will avoid the problems experienced by small boats in rough water. The wind resistance will slow the boat down less than water crashing over the sides in rough conditions.

Generally, there are two predominant boat shapes: the 'U' and the 'V'. The 'U'-shape with its flatter bottom provides better stability and is more suitable for the less experienced sculler. The 'V'-shape is theoretically faster with its lower wetted surface area. However, a certain amount of experience is needed to be able to scull and balance it. It is recommended to seek the advice of experienced coaches and boat-builders about the most appropriate boat shape.

Construction Materials and Weight

There are few boat-builders left making timber boats. Materials used for boat construction have moved from timber to fibreglass, honeycomb, carbon and composites.

The minimum weight for a single scull is 14kg. For an international racing scull, the requirement will be for a stiff boat within 200g of this weight. This will mean using a considerable amount of carbon to keep the weight down and to maximize its strength and stiffness. This will be the most expensive type of boat. However, those who do not have the same performance aspirations might like to consider a fibreglass scull that may be heavier and not quite as stiff, but will nevertheless suit their needs.

Fittings and riggers also come in various levels of sophistication. A 'winged' rigger reduces wind resistance and moves the rigger blocks away from the hull of the boat, so that waves do not hit them in rough water.

Quality

Always look for boats that are finished well. A sculling boat is a considerable outlay of money, so you should inspect the scull prior to delivery and make sure that the boat has been finished to your satisfaction. Always check that what you ordered is what you are receiving. Also check that:

- there is no damage to the hull, either by extraction from the mould or travel;
- any joins have been well sealed;
- all safety features are satisfactory;
- the fit and range of the rigging is what you ordered;
- the fittings are even across the boat;
- the accessories you ordered have been fitted.

Boat-Builder's Reputation, Reliability and After-Sales Service

A successful boat-builder who builds consistently good-quality boats will have a reputation for consistent quality. When you have narrowed down the types of boat you are considering, you should ask around among fellow scullers and find out what they think of the different boats. Make sure you also ask about after-sales service and whether a repair service is provided if the boat is damaged.

MAINTENANCE

Once you have bought the boat you must look after it. A cover, preferably in a light colour so that it will not attract the heat, will keep the boat clean and free of road grime when transporting. Never leave the boat in a wet cover. The dampness will cause mould and damage the boat's surface. Most boats never receive the attention they deserve. Ideally, a boat should be washed down with fresh water after every use and dried with chamois leather. In addition, it should be washed with soap and water and dried with chamois leather every week, and polished with a quality marine or car polish every month. This routine will ensure that the boat remains in excellent overall condition and maintains its glossy hull. When sculling in salt water,

---

Sculls

When selecting a scull remember to consider:

- shape;
- size;
- material;
- reputation and reliability of the manufacturer.

131

the boat and blades have to be thoroughly washed to prevent corrosion and damage to the scull and its fittings. Fittings should be regularly checked and cleaned. Prior to racing, always check that the nuts and bolts are tight but not over-tightened.

Sculling Blades

Although many variations are available, most sculls come with adjustable lengths that allow for flexibility with rigging. It is advisable to buy adjustable-length sculls, so that you have the ability to change your rig easily. The sculls' shafts are made from carbon and come in various levels of stiffness. The developing athlete might like to consider a softer shaft to the seasoned sculler. The stiffer shaft is less forgiving and may apply more force from the sculler to the blade. If the sculler has only a limited training background, the stiffer shafts may provide increased force through the trunk and lead to rib injuries. Sculls also come with various grip sizes. It is important that you use handles that are not too big for you, which may lead to difficulties with feathering and squaring the blade. Spoon shapes can vary and there is not a lot of hard evidence that one is better than the other. You should experiment with different shapes and go with the one that feels most effective. As with boat selection, if you think you have the most effective-shaped sculls, then you probably have.

ACCESSORIES

The beauty about sculling is that you rely on no-one else. You also have the ability to travel easily with your boat using a sculling rack on your car. Make sure that your car is of a suitable length to take the rack and scull, and that it is within the limits of the law – make sure you check the regulations. Tie down both ends of the scull and tape a red flag to the back of the boat. There are many other accessories that can help to monitor and to assist you in your quest to improve. Some of the following may help. Most are available through the Internet, magazines and at regattas.

Pace coaches and other devices that measure rate and speed are extremely useful in monitoring training. Pace coaches record the number of times the seat passes over a magnetic sensor to measure how many strokes a minute you are rating. The speed coach comes with an impellor that attaches to the bottom of the boat, a sensor on the hull picks up the speed and it is displayed by a compact unit that fits on the foot stretcher. The latest generation of these can be downloaded onto a laptop for analysis. This, combined with a heart-rate monitor, provides the basic tools you need to monitor your training. You can then monitor your physiological effort through the heart rate and assess it against your boat speed and rate. Satellite technology is now starting to challenge the traditional wired pace coach units. GPS systems are now coming into the marketplace; they are able to wirelessly link the coach with the sculler. The coach can be on the bank and receive the sculler's location, speed, rate and heart rate in real-time.

There are also bio-mechanical feedback systems available. These are becoming more robust as technology progresses and they can provide stroke-power profiles, boat acceleration and velocity traces, as well as stroke angles and rates. Video technology is also moving quite fast. Video goggles that are available for home entertainment use often come with a wireless remote system that can be connected to a digital video camera. Video goggles provide you with immediate visual feedback while sculling.

Video feedback is still a valuable tool to provide you with technical feedback. Many digital cameras available are small, lightweight, and quite robust, and have an extremely good picture quality. Ideally, select a camera that has slow motion, jog and frame-by-frame functions. When filming, coaches should follow some basic guidelines:

- use the video in good water and weather conditions;
- plan what you are going to video;
- wear plain clothes;
- video from a launch and use an experienced driver;

- video at least five strokes in each position:
- side on with the sculler in full frame (both sides);
- side on with the sculler and blades in full frame (both sides);
- side on with cross-over of hands in full frame;
- rear view with the sculler in full frame.

CHAPTER 12
The Last Word

I hope that this book has explained some of the essential elements of sculling and that you will be able to adapt them to your own situation. Sculling can be done either on your own or as a member of a crew. As a single-sculler, you control your own destiny, relying on no-one else for success or failure. Crew scullers combine together for a common goal and purpose, sharing their experiences, successes and failures. You can participate in the sport either as a recreational sculler or with the ambition to compete. However, regardless of whether you scull alone or as a member of a crew, and at whatever level you scull, you will always be striving to make your next stroke better than your last. In a single-scull you will always be searching for the feeling and sound of the boat's run, as well as the sound of the blade entering the water. In a crew boat, you will search for the same feelings and sounds but must also concentrate on perfecting the synchronistic timing that crew sculling demands. This is the same in recreational as in racing crews.

International single-sculling racing brings out the toughest and hardest athletes. They must enjoy their own company, as this is essential for single sculling. Although they win and lose on their own merits, there is a shared respect for the battles they have raced.

Martin Cross, an Olympic gold medallist and national sculling representative observed that:

> ...the successful sculler's need of proving himself on his own is different from a rower.

He has a need to prove something about himself for himself and the single is the vehicle for them. There is a brotherhood in scullers around the world; it is based on recognition by peers.

Peter Shakespear, development manager for the ARA and former Australian team coach, described how he witnessed three scullers having a drink at a bar at the World Championships in 1989 at Bled, Yugoslavia. They were Pertti Karppinen and Thomas Lange, winners of the Olympic singles title at the Moscow, Los Angeles and Seoul Olympics, and the man who had come second to them at those three games, Peter-Michael Kolbe. Shakespear saw it as the young German, Lange, receiving recognition and acceptance into the elite brotherhood that only a few scullers have achieved. Lange was about to be elected chair; he went on to defend his Olympic title in Barcelona. Shakespear is also matter-of-fact about the mindset of the single-sculler: 'Too much is talked about the sculler's mentality, of course they're individuals. If you row a fast single scull why row someone who is not as good as you?'

Scullers do not have to be the solitary types; in fact most end up in sculling crews at some stage and so benefit from the experience of shared goals and camaraderie, as well as shared success and setbacks. However, single-scullers develop their own style that can be difficult to merge into a successful synchronized unit. After seasons of independence, it can be hard for a single-sculler to perform as part of a crew.

The rhythm and power of a successful sculling crew can be amazing to watch. As scullers have two oars to the rower's one, they have a greater blade surface area to propel them and can move extremely quickly. Often a quad-scull will beat an eight during racing starts.

David Tanner, the ARAs international manager, saw the British men's double-scull of Chris Baillieu and Mike Hart winning the 1977 World Championships as a turning point for modern British scullers and rowers. By winning, Baillieu and Hart demonstrated to all other scullers and rowers in Britain at the time that they could believe, not just in the possibility of competing but in leading the world. Another breakthrough for Britain came in 2001 when Mathew Langridge won the World Junior Single Sculling title. Tanner is hoping that the World Class Start Programme will develop more young athletes to follow Langridge's example.

Britain's rowers and scullers have a proud record, having won gold medals at the last six Olympic Games and many medals in international regattas, and World Championships in lightweight and open men's and women's sculling events. There are many national, regional and club events for scullers to enjoy and participate in at every level. Thirteen-year-old Royal Docks Rowing Club Harry McCarthy sculls because he loves being:

...out on the water, the feeling of the boat up and running is really good. I have made loads of friends – they are all friends down here [at the Royal Docks Rowing Club]. I love racing but do not like the training! I raced at Maidstone last year in the J13's [under 13 years of age] in the Head Race, I had a really good row I got the boat up and moving, all the coaches and my dad were running along the bank yelling – 'we can see the finish, push away, you're doing really well, let's go.' It was really cool and I won!

GLOSSARY

Blade Spoon on the end of the oar's shaft that is placed in the water.

Blade work Path of the scull's blade both in and out of the water during the sculling stroke.

Bow Forward section of the boat. In crew boats the rowing position closest to the bow is known as the bow seat.

Catch Blade entering the water, also known as placement.

Cockpit Area of the boat where the sculler or rower sits.

Collar Part of the oar that rests against the outrigger's swivel.

Coxless boat A boat without a coxswain, steered by the rower or sculler.

Coxswain Steersman.

Double-scull Two-man rowing boat, also known as a double. The scullers have two oars each.

Drive phase Propulsive phase of the stroke.

Ergometer Rowing machine.

Feathering Rolling of the blade on to the sill of the swivel with the blade being parallel to the water. Occurs at the finish of the stroke.

Finish Exit of the blade from the water.

Foot stretcher Where the sculler's feet are attached to the boat.

Port Right-hand side of the boat as you sit in it, also known as the strokeside.

Quadruple- or quad-scull A four-man rowing boat, also known as a quad. The scullers have two oars each.

Recovery phase Part of the stroke cycle where the sculler moves from releasing the blades from the water at the finish to placing the blades in the water at the catch.

Rowing Propelling the boat by holding one oar with both hands.

Sculling Propelling the boat by holding an oar in each hand.

Sculls A pair of sculling oars.

Single-scull One-man rowing boat, propelled by holding an oar in each hand, also known as a single or scull.

Slip Extent to which the blade slips in the water without providing effective force against it as it enters at the catch and leaves at the finish.

Squaring Blade is squared from the feathered position in preparation for placement into the water at the catch.

Starboard Left-hand side of the boat as you sit in it, also known as bowside.

Stern Aft section of the boat. In crew boats the rowing position closest to the stern is known as the stroke position.

Swivel Part of the boat's outrigger that holds the oar.

FURTHER READING

BOOKS

Alter, M., *Sport Stretch* (Human Kinetics, 1998)

Bull, S., *Sport Psychology: A Self-Help Guide* (The Crowood Press, 1991)

Bull, S. *et al.*, *The Mental Game Plan* (Sports Dynamics, 1999)

Delavier, F., *Strength Training Anatomy* (Human Kinetics, 2001)

Dodd, C., *Henley Royal Regatta*, 150th Anniversary Edition (Stanley Paul & Co., 1989)

Dodd, C., *The Story of World Rowing* (Stanley Paul & Co., 1992)

FISA, *Be a Coach* (International Rowing Federation, 2002)

Hawley, J. and Burke, L., *Peak P erformance* (Allen & Unwin, 1998)

Herberger, E. *et al.*, Rowing rudern. *The GDR text of Oarsmanship*, 4th edn (Sport Books Publisher, 1989)

McArthur, J., *High Performance Rowing* (The Crowood Press, 1997)

McNeely, E. and Royle, M., *Skilful Rowing* (Meyer & Meyer Sport, 2002)

Orlick, T., *Psyching for Sport* (Human Kinetics, 1986)

Orlick, T., *In Pursuit of Excellence*, 2nd edn (Human Kinetics, 1990)

Orlick, T., *Embracing Your Potential* (Human Kinetics, 1998)

Peterson, L. and Renstrom, P., *Sports Injuries*, 3rd edn (Martin Dunitz, 2001)

Whitehead, I., *James Renforth of Gateshead: Champion Sculler of the World* (Tyne Bridge Publishing, 2004)

PAPERS

Baudouin, A. and Hawkins, D., 'A Biomechanical Review of Factors Affecting Rowing Performance', *Br. J. Sports Med.* (2002, vol.36, pp.396–402)

Christiansen, E. and Kanstrup, I.L., 'Increased Risk of Stress Fractures of the Ribs in Elite Rowers', *Scand. Med. Sci. Sports* (1997, vol.7, pp.49–52)

Hagerman, F.C., 'Applied Physiology of Rowing', *Sports Med.* (1984, vol.1, pp.303–326)

Hartmann, U. *et al.*, 'Peak Force, Velocity and Power during Five and Ten Maximal Rowing Ergometer Strokes by World Class Female and Male Rowers', *Int. J. Sports Med.* (1993, vol.14, pp.S42–S45)

Hickey, G.J., Fricker, P.A., and McDonald, W.A., 'Injuries to Elite Rowers Over A Ten-Year Period', *Med. Sci. Sports Exer.* (1997, vol.29, pp.1567–1572)

Holt, P.J.E., *et al.*, 'Rowing Technique: The Influence of Fatigue on Anteroposterior Movements and Force Production', *Int. J. Sports Med.* (2003, vol.24, pp.597–602)

Hosea, T.M., *et al.*, 'Rowing Injuries', *Postgrad. Adv. Sports Med.* (1989, vol.3, pp.1–16)

Howell, D.W., 'Musculoskeletal Profile and Incidence of Musculoskeletal Injuries in Light-weight Women Rowers', *Am. J. Sports Med.* (1984, vol.12, pp.278–282)

Kleshnev, V., Australian Rowing (2001, vol.24, no.1)

Lamb, D.H., 'A Kinematic Comparison of Ergometer and On-Water Rowing', *Am. J. Sports Med.* (1989, vol.7, pp.367–373)

Mahler, D.A., Nelson, M.S. and Hagerman, F.C., 'Mechanical and Physiological Evaluation of Exercise Performance in Elite National Rowers', *JAMA* (vol.252, no.4, pp.496–499)

Martin, T.P. and Bernfield, J.S., 'Effect of Stroke Rate on Velocity of a Rowing Shell', *Med. Sci. Sports Exerc.* (1980, vol.12, pp.250–256)

McGregor, A.H., Anderton, L. and Gedroyc, W.M.W., 'Asymmetries in the Trunks of Elite Oarsmen', *Br. J. Sports Med.* (2002, vol.36, pp.214–217)

McGregor, A.H., Anderton, L. and Gedroyc, W.M.W., 'The Assessment of Intersegmental Motion and Pelvic Tilt in Elite Oarsmen using Interventional Magnetic Resonance Imaging', *Med. & Sci. in Sports & Exercise* (2002, vol.34, no.7, pp.1143–1149)

McGregor, A.H., Bull, A.M.J. and Byng-Maddick, R., 'A Comparison of Rowing Technique at Different Stroke Rates – a Description of Sequencing, Force Production and Kinematics', *Int. J. Sports Med.* (2004, vol.25, pp.465–470)

McGregor, A.H., Hill, A. and Grewar, J., 'Trunk Strength Patterns in Elite Rowers', *Isokinetics and Exercise Science* (2004, vol.12, pp.253–261)

Parkin S. *et al.*, 'Do Sweep Stroke Oarsmen have Asymmetries in the Strength of their Back and Leg Muscles?', *J. Sport Sci.* (2001, vol.19, pp.521–526)

Roy S.H., *et al.*, 'Fatigue, Recovery and LBP in Varsity Rowers', *Med. Sci. Sports Exerc.* (1990, vol.22, pp.463–469)

Shepherd, R.J., 'Science and Medicine of Rowing: A Review', *J. Sports Sci.* (1998, vol.16, pp.603–620)

Shiang, T.-Y. and Tsai, C.-B., 'The Kinetic Characteristics of Rowing Movements', In Haake, S. J. (eds) *The Engineering in Sport* (Blackwell Science, 1998), pp.219–224

Smith, R.M., and Spinks, W.L., 'Discriminate Analysis of Biomechanical Differences between Novice, Good and Elite Rowers', *J. Sports Sci.* (1995, vol.13, pp.377–385)

Wajswelner, H. *et al.*, 'Muscle Action and Stress on the Ribs in Rowing', *Phys. Ther. Sport* (2000, vol.1, pp.75–84)

Wing, A.M. and Woodburn, C., 'The Coordination and Consistency of Rowers in A Racing Eight', *J. Sports Sci.* (1995, vol.13, pp.187–197)

APPENDIX I SAMPLE TRAINING SESSIONS

Training Zone	Training Session	Recovery Between Sets	Training Zone Stroke Rate	Training Zone Speed Range	Heart Rate Range (% of max)
U3	1×120 minutes	Only to turn boat around and rehydrate	<18	<70%	65–75%
U3	4 × 30 minutes	Only to turn boat around and rehydrate	<18	<70%	65–75%
U3	120–180 minutes (bike riding)	Only to rehydrate and refuel			65–75%
U2	60–110 minutes	Only to turn boat around and rehydrate	17–18	70–76%	65–75%
U2	100 minutes including 40 minutes of 2-minute stroke rate changes. Rates should alternate between 16 and 18 strokes per minute	Only to turn boat around and rehydrate	16–18	70–76%	65–75%
U2	100 minutes including 60 minutes of 5-minute stroke rate changes. Rates should alternate between 16 and 18 strokes per minute	Only to turn boat around and rehydrate	16–18	70–76%	65–75%
U1	3 × 20 minutes with stroke rate changes every 5 minutes Set 1. 5 minutes at rate 19/21/23/19 Set 2. 5 minutes at rate 23/21/19/23 Set 3. 5 minutes at rate 23/19/23/19	5 minutes	19–23	77–82%	70–80%
U1	3 × 20 minutes with stroke rate changes every 2 minutes Set 1. 2 minutes at rate 19/21/23/19 Set 2. 2 minutes at rate 23/21/19/23 Set 3. 2 minutes at rate 23/19/23/19	5 minutes	19–23	77–82%	70–80%
U1	2 × 40 minutes with stroke rate changes every 5 minutes between 19 and 23 strokes per minute Set 1. 5 minute steps at rate 19/21/23/19/21/23/19/21 Set 2. 5 minute steps at rate 23/21/19/23/21/19/23/21	10 minutes	19–23	77–82%	70–80%
AT	3 × 20 minutes at set stroke rates 24 and 26. Set 1. R24 Set 2. R26 Set 3. R24	10 minutes	24–28	82–86%	80–85%

Training Zone	Training Session	Recovery Between Sets	Training Zone Stroke Rate	Training Zone Speed Range	Heart Rate Range (% of max)
AT	3 × 15 minutes with 5 minute stroke rate steps between 24 and 28 Set 1. 5 minute steps at rate 24/26/28 Set 2. 5 minute steps at rate 26/24/26 Set 3. 5 minute steps at rate 28/26/28	10–15 minutes	24–28	82–86%	80–85%
AT	4 × 2,000 metres Stroke rates should step at 500m/1,000m/500m Set 1. R24/26/28 Set 2. R26/24/26 Set 3. R28/26/28	10–12 minutes	24–28	82–86%	80–85%
TPT	4 × 7 minutes The 7 minutes is broken into steps of 3 minutes, 2 minutes and 2 minutes. There is an increase in stroke rate at each of the steps. The stroke rate in all pieces is 28/30/32	7–10 minutes	28–36	87–95%	85–95%
TPT	4 × 4 minutes The 4 minutes is broken into steps of 2 minutes, 1 minute and 1 minute. There is an increase in stroke rate at each of the steps. Set 1 & 2. R28/30/32 Set 3 & 4. R30/32/34	4–8 minutes	28–36	87–95%	85–95%
TPT	4 × 4 minutes The 4 minutes is broken down into steps of 1 minute, 2 minutes and 1 minute. There is an increase in rate at each of the steps. Set 1 & 2. R 30/28/30 Set 3 & 4. R 32/30/32	4–8 minutes	28–36	87–95%	85–95%
AN	12 × 1 minute Each minute is undertaken at race pace	1–1.5 minutes	36+	100%+	Max
AN	4 × (12 strokes on/ 20 strokes off) each 12 stroke piece is undertaken at race pace	10–15 minutes	36+	100%+	Max

APPENDIX II TWO-WEEK TAPER

Day	Aim	Session 1	Aim	Session 2
Sunday	Technical focus and physical warm up	Pre-race row	Race	
Saturday	Technical focus and physical warm up	Pre-race row	Race	
Friday Days to racing 1	Maximum speed and race pace	2 × 250m: 1 × standing start 1 × mid pace	First ten strokes of race practice	Start Practice
Thursday Days to racing 2	Specific race practice	2 × 500m: 1 × standing start 1 × mid pace	Recovery and regeneration	Off
Wednesday Days to racing 3	Rhythm and aerobic base maintenance	U2 Training	First twenty strokes of race practice	Start Practice
Tuesday Days to racing 4	Specific race practice and race-plan rehearsal	2 × 1,000m: 1 × 1,000m from a standing start (practising the first 1,000m of the race) 1 × 1,000m from a running start (practising the second 1,000m of the race)	Recovery, regeneration and technique	U2 Training
Monday Days to racing 5	Rhythm and aerobic base maintenance	U2 Training	Alactic training to promote moving at speed	6 × 12 strokes at racing speed/20 strokes off) *alactic anaerobic*
Sunday Days to racing 6	Recovery and regeneration	Off	Recovery and regeneration	Off
Saturday Days to racing 7	Specific race practice and race-plan rehearsal 1 × 1,500m from a standing start (1st 1,500m of race plan) 1 × 500m from a running start (last 500m of race plan)	1 × 1,500m/1 × 500m	Recovery, regeneration and technique	U2 Training
Friday Days to racing 8	Rhythm and aerobic base maintenance	U2 Training	First ten strokes of race practice	Start Practice

Day	Aim	Session 1	Aim	Session 2
Thursday Days to racing 9	Alactic training to promote moving at speed	2 × (6 × 12 strokes at racing/20 strokes off) *alactic anaerobic*	Strength retention	Weights
Wednesday Days to racing 10	Rhythm and specific aerobic training and race-plan rehearsal	U1 Training 3 × 2,000m R23/19/21/23	Recovery, regeneration and technique	U2 Training
Tuesday Days to racing 11	Alactic training to promote moving at speed	2 × (6 × 12 strokes at racing/20 strokes off) *alactic anaerobic*	Strength retention	Weights
Monday Days to racing 12	Rhythm and aerobic base maintenance	U2 Training	Recovery, regeneration and technique	U2 Training
Sunday Days to racing 13	Recovery and regeneration	Off	Recovery and regeneration	Off
Saturday Days to racing 14	Build rhythm and distance per stroke	2 × 2,000m: 1 × 2,000m rate step each 500m R22/24/26/28 1 × 2,000m rate step each 500m R24/26/28/30	Recovery, regeneration and technique	U2 Training

APPENDIX III WEIGHTS TESTING PROTOCOL

Warm up with 10 repetitions below starting weight prior to each exercise.

Level	Power Clean	Back Squat	Bench Pull
A	20	40	20
B	25	45	25
C	30	50	30
D	35	55	35
E	40	60	40
F	45	65	45
G	50	70	50
H	55	75	55
I	60	80	60
J	65	85	65
K	70	90	70
L	75	95	75
M	80	100	80
N	85	105	85
O	90	110	90
P	95	115	95
Q	100	120	100
R	105	125	105
S	110	130	110
T	115	135	115
U	120	140	120
V	125	145	125
W	130	150	130
X	135	155	135
Y	140	160	140
Z	145	165	145

Rules

Power Clean	Form and back position must be held to count lift
Squat	Squat to 90 degrees holding back position
Bench Pull	Chin, chest and legs stay on bench during pull
Cadence	Rhythmical – one lift at least every three seconds
Number of lifts at each level	12
	Record level/number of successful lifts/reason for failure

^ = slow lifts

x = failed

o = no attempt

INDEX